Voices for Justice

Academic Monograph No. 17

The Academic Monograph series is designed to encourage publication of specialised manuscripts of interest to the wider community.

Voices for Justice

Church, Law and State in New Zealand

Jonathan Boston
Alan Cameron

The Dunmore Press Ltd

First Published in 1994
by
The Dunmore Press Limited
P.O.Box 5115
Palmertson North
New Zealand

ISBN 0 86469 209 9

Text: Times 10/12
Page Layout: June Mercer
Printer: The Dunmore Printing Company Ltd, Palmerston North

Contents

Acknowledgements

Numerous people have commented on chapters and assisted in various other ways with the publication of this book. The editors and authors would particularly like to thank Bill Atkin, Geoff Bertram, Les Brighton, Gillian Cameron, Michael Duncan, Jeff Greenman, Mary Hutchinson, Michael Irwin, Penny Jamieson, Peter Lineham, Raymond Pelly, Richard Randerson, Adrian Whale, Cardinal Tom Williams, and Marcellin Wilson. The editors would also like to thank the Association for Christian Scholarship, the VUW Anglican Chaplaincy and the VUW Ecumenical Chaplaincy for their financial assistance towards the costs of the seminar in late 1993 upon which most of the chapters in this book are based.

Preface

The essays contained in this volume arose out of papers presented at a one-day symposium held at Victoria University of Wellington in late 1993. The purpose of the symposium was to provide an opportunity for considered responses to the church leaders' *Social Justice Statement* issued in July of that year. A range of people were invited to the symposium, including academics, policy advisers and those involved in drafting the *Statement.* A deliberate effort was made to involve people from a range of theological and philosophical perspectives. Five people were invited to contribute papers on themes relevant to the *Statement*, and each paper was commented on by a respondent. The contributors were then asked to revise their papers taking into account the views of the respondents and other participants at the symposium. The revisions varied from relatively minor (Chapters 3, 4 and 5) to substantial (Chapters 2 and 6).

Two motivations prompted this publication. First, there is a dearth of serious, in-depth analyses of contemporary economic and social policy issues in New Zealand, especially contributions from a distinctively Christian perspective. One of the aims of this volume is to help fill this vacuum. Second, the *Social Justice Statement* represents a significant contribution from the leaders of the Christian community on a number of vital contemporary issues relating to the nature of a just society. Without question, it deserves careful scrutiny – from Christians and non-Christians alike.

While this volume seeks to provide such a scrutiny, we recognise that the coverage is by no means comprehensive or complete. Many aspects of social justice have not been explored, or have been addressed only fleetingly. For example, there is no detailed empirical analysis of the increase in poverty and inequality in New Zealand in recent years. Nor is there an assessment of how the churches and their various social service agencies have responded to the growing evidence of human deprivation. Whilst Christian perspectives on the role of the state, and the manner in which the church conducts itself in the realm of public affairs, have been addressed, more could be said about the relationship between the state and church as social institutions. Likewise, this volume lacks a specifically Maori 'voice' or a distinctively feminist perspective. Despite these limitations, it is our hope that the material presented here will provide a focus for the continuing debate over the issues raised in the *Social Justice Statement*.

All the contributors to this volume share the conviction that adherence to Christian beliefs involves a commitment to social justice, and that this commitment must be expressed in both deeds and words. While the contributors are united in these convictions, their views on what constitutes a just society are by no means identical. It is thus entirely appropriate that this volume has been entitled *Voices for Justice*.

In Chapter 1, Jonathan Boston provides background to the *Statement*, including the various contributions of the different churches, and comments on, and responds to, some of the criticisms that have been made of the *Statement*. He expresses some concerns about the *Statement's* apparent adoption of 'middle axioms' as the vehicle for the churches' contribution to the formulation of public policy. Further, he argues that the churches should not refrain from commenting on so-called 'technical' matters or detailed policy matters, especially where these impinge on important issues of a moral nature.

Alan Cameron, in Chapter 2, examines the Catholic contribution to the *Statement.* He adopts a Reformational perspective little known in this part of the world. After providing an outline of this perspective and its conceptions of law, justice and state, Cameron applies this approach to a critique of the concepts of law, justice and the state underlying Catholic teaching on social justice. In particular, he examines, and criticises aspects of, the concept of the common good and its associated principles of subsidiarity and supplementation which feature in the *Statement.* He relates these criticisms to a perceived lack of precision in the *Statement's* definition of social justice. Nevertheless, he finds a considerable degree of affinity between the Catholic teaching on the common good and subsidiarity, on the one hand, and the Reformational social principle of 'sphere sovereignty', on the other. He sees each being able to benefit from the insights of the other in their attempts to articulate a Christian political philosophy and to address issues of social justice.

Chapter 3 contains Jonathan Boston's second contribution to the book. In it he grapples with the difficult question of the relation between love and justice. First, he observes how the *Statement's* approach to issues of social justice rests on a view that emphasises the importance of both love and justice.

Neighbour love certainly has a role in public life, although it must normally find expression through the medium of justice. He then examines, and briefly critiques, three different positions concerning the relationship between love and justice espoused by some leading twentieth century theologians. Of these positions, Boston prefers the view that love and justice are different but inseparable. He argues that this approach is implicit, if not explicit, in the *Statement*. However, he expresses concern that the *Statement* fails to address some of the practical difficulties involved in giving institutional expression to the requirements of love and justice. In company with Cameron in Chapter 2, he is also critical of the *Statement's* rather vague definition of social justice.

Chapter 4 tackles a critical issue underlying all attempts to provide a Christian perspective on issues of social justice. Christopher Marshall examines the role of the Bible as an ethical-religious guide and the appropriate hermeneutic principles for its interpretation. Rejecting the idea of a single method for exploring the moral implications of Scripture, he identifies a number of possible hermeneutical approaches. Of special interest in relation to the ethical concerns of the *Statement* is the method which views the Bible as having a role in the formation of individual character and community. Having evaluated the strengths and weaknesses of each of the hermeneutical approaches, Marshall relates them to the concerns of the *Statement*. Along with all the other contributors to the book, Marshall affirms a deep respect for the Bible as a normative guide for the life of both individual Christians and the Christian community.

Ruth Smithies is the contributor of Chapter 5. She presents an overview of the developments in Catholic social teaching from the encyclical *Rerum Novarum* (1891) up to the present day. Amongst those developments noted are the greater emphasis given to the importance of the Bible, the widening of the concept of sin to include structural sin, and the widening of the concept of poverty to include lack of education, knowledge and know-how. Smithies provides helpful background on, and explanations of, some of the central concepts upon which the *Social Justice Statement* is based. These concepts include the common good, subsidiarity and solidarity (or supplementation), which are critiqued in Chapter 2.

Of all the chapters, Chapter 6 is most likely to evoke strong responses, both inside and outside Christian circles. Petrus Simons presents a critique of some of the fundamental theoretical assumptions underlying the economic and social policies of recent governments in New Zealand and finds them seriously wanting. In particular, he challenges the Treasury's view of humanity and society. He also criticises the individualism of its contractual model of human relationships, and the over-emphasis on the idea of human freedom and reason. The Treasury's approach to social and economic policy is seen as a major contributor to some of the current social problems of unemployment, inequality and violence.

It is our hope that this collection of essays will help to foster amongst Christians and the wider community informed debate and dialogue on the nature of a just society and the respective responsibilities of individuals, voluntary groups and the state. If this purpose is achieved, it will be continuing what the church leaders have begun in their *Social Justice Statement.*

Jonathan Boston
Alan Cameron
August 1994
Wellington

Chapter 1

Christianity in the Public Square

The Churches and Social Justice

Jonathan Boston

I will make justice the measure and righteousness the plumb line.

(Isaiah 28:17)

The Church Leaders' Social Justice Initiative

Unlike many countries, the relationship between church and state in New Zealand has rarely been the subject of significant political controversy. Nor have specifically religious or denominational issues played a dominant role in defining the contours of the political landscape or in galvanising political action. Broadly speaking, most Christian denominations have seen their mission primarily in terms of evangelism and the provision of educational and social services; their focus has been more on individual salvation rather than social transformation and political reform. This is not to suggest that the churches in New Zealand have been silent on the broader questions of social justice, human rights and the common good. Pietism and quietism have certainly had their champions, but they have not been the only, or even the dominant, strands of theological opinion. Hence, it has been common for individual Christians to be actively involved in political parties and public affairs. Church leaders, together with the Public Questions Committees (or their equivalents) of the various denominations, have regularly commented on controversial policy matters, whether the narrower, so-called 'moral' issues such as abortion and homosexuality, or the broader (and equally moral) issues of economic and social policy, biculturalism and the Treaty of Waitangi, international relations and defence. It has also been common for church councils, assemblies and synods to pass motions on important matters of public concern (e.g. the Vietnam war, sporting contacts with South Africa, the ethics of nuclear deterrence, and so forth).

Yet while individual Christians and church leaders have long participated in the political process, seeing this as part of their Christian calling and democratic responsibility, and while the quest for a just society (interpreted in many and varied ways) has been a central component of Christian teaching, the various denominations have not, as a rule, chosen to co-operate in their pursuit of common social or political objectives. Independent, rather than co-ordinated, inter-denominational action has been the norm.[1] In the early 1990s this traditional mode of political engagement changed significantly. Prompted by the increasing evidence of poverty, social distress, and financial hardship, and spurred on by the growing pressures facing Christian social service agencies, the leaders of the major denominations became much more active and persistent opponents of the existing policy regime.[2] Indeed, following the substantial cuts to welfare benefits in April 1991, the churches emerged as amongst the National government's most vociferous, penetrating and effective critics.

The level of concern within the churches over poverty and unemployment, and the general direction of government policy was such that in 1992, at the request of the New Zealand Council of Christian Social Services, the leaders of ten denominations representing most of the Christian church embarked upon a co-operative project to promote the cause of social justice.[3] The ten churches involved were the Apostolic, Anglican, Associated Churches of Christ, Baptist, Catholic, Lutheran, Methodist, Presbyterian, Religious Society of Friends (Quakers), and the Salvation Army.[4] All the leaders of these churches participated in, and contributed to, the project in various ways. Nevertheless, it is probably fair to say that the most influential figures were Cardinal Tom Williams (the head of the Roman Catholic Church) and Rev Keith Rowe (the head of the Methodist Church). In developing their strategy and preparing their various statements, the church leaders were assisted by a small secretariat comprising Dr Ruth Smithies (the Project Officer for Cardinal Williams) and Helen Wilson (the Research Officer for the Public Questions Committee of the Methodist and Presbyterian Churches). Significant contributions were also made by a number of other people, most notably Rev Richard Randerson, the Social Responsibility Commissioner for the Anglican Church.

The 'Social Justice Initiative', as it became known, culminated in the joint preparation and release of two public statements, a *Statement of Intent*, issued on 31 January 1993, and a subsequent *Social Justice Statement* issued on 11 July 1993. A book was also published in parallel with the latter document, *Making Choices: Social Justice for Our Times*. This consisted of study material and worship resources for congregational use, together with 11 background papers dealing with key policy issues (e.g. education, employment, health, housing, the Treaty of Waitangi, social welfare and taxation). The papers were written by policy specialists drawn from the spectrum of churches participating in the Social Justice Initiative. The church leaders declared 11 July 1993 to be 'Social Justice Sunday'. Individual congregations were urged to reflect on the *Social Justice Statement* and the issues it raised in their church services.

The historical and political significance of these church leaders' Statements must not be underestimated. Remarkably, the release of the Statements witnessed the first occasion, certainly in New Zealand's history and possibly also in the history of the Christian church generally, when the leaders of all the major denominations have put their names to documents dealing with matters of social and political theology. Never before, in other words, had such an ecumenical exercise been attempted, let alone been brought to fruition. Nor had church leaders representing such a wide range of theological positions previously reached agreement on the nature of social justice and the respective responsibilities of individuals, families, voluntary organisations and the state.

Politically, too, the Statements were important. They both generated lively public debate, not to mention vigorous controversy within the various churches represented.[5] The media gave both Statements considerable attention. Most of the major daily newspapers commented on them in editorials, and carried articles assessing their merits. In some respects this was surprising, particularly given the increasingly marginal role of the church in New Zealand society and the limited acceptance within the policy community of the relevance of theology to public affairs.

Although essentially non-partisan in nature, both Statements were almost universally, and accurately, interpreted as being critical of the National government's policy direction, especially in the arena of social policy. Not unnaturally, therefore, the Statements were welcomed by the main opposition parties, Labour and the Alliance, but found little support from within the ranks of the government and its supporters. At best, National MPs offered cautious acceptance of the principles enunciated in the Statements. The more common response, however, was negative, if not hostile. Those National MPs with church affiliations were particularly annoyed at the implicit, if not explicit, criticisms of their policy approach. With an election to fight at the end of 1993, the government was acutely aware of the potential political damage which the criticisms of the church leaders could cause. It consequently took various measures to neutralise the negative political impact of the Statements. On the one hand, both Statements were subjected to trenchant criticisms. In some cases the integrity and competency of the church leaders was also challenged. On the other hand, senior ministers, including the Prime Minister, Jim Bolger, met with the church leaders to discuss the government's social policies and explore solutions to the growing problems of poverty. While these discussions bore little tangible fruit, the small increase in the level of family support payments in the 1993 Budget (for low-income families with teenagers) can be attributed, at least in part, to the Social Justice Initiative.

But what exactly did the two Statements say? What principles did they enunciate? What responses did they provoke? What lessons do the Statements provide for the way in which the churches should seek to contribute to public debate? In particular, what is the proper role of theology in guiding the formulation of public policy? This chapter considers these and related questions. Subsequent chapters explore some of the wider theological and policy issues raised by the Statements, including the relationship between justice and the law, the relationship between justice and love, and the foundations for Christian ethics.

The Statements

Both the *Statement of Intent* issued in January 1993 and the subsequent *Social Justice Statement* are brief documents, the first being around 1,000 words, the latter fewer than 3,000 words. Both are concerned largely with matters of political theology rather than political philosophy. Both deal more with general principles than with specific policies. Both are reformist in tone and content. They endorse the market economy rather than centralised planning, but a market economy appropriately regulated in the interests of social justice and the common good. Both were written primarily to provide theological guidance for church members on the nature of social justice and their responsibilities as citizens. It was recognised, however, that they would attract a much wider public interest, and it was certainly intended that the principles they enunciated would be applied to the current political context.

More specifically, the *Statement of Intent* made it abundantly clear that the church leaders were deeply troubled by the negative impact of recent economic and social policy changes on many groups, especially the poor. As the *Statement* puts it:

> We recognise that recent governments have sought to address the nation's serious economic difficulties, and we realise that any solution to our economic problems will cause pain. Our deep concern is that the pain has not been shared fairly. People are being marginalised and live in despair and anger, with no hope for their future. Their plight must be addressed now. A basic moral test of society is how its most vulnerable members are faring. This is not a new insight. It is the lesson of the parable of the Last Judgement ...[6]

Emphasising that their intention was not 'to be party political' or 'to cast blame', the church leaders urged their members to take seriously their responsibilities as Christian citizens. With the forthcoming election in mind, they argued that all followers of Jesus Christ should examine the policies advanced by political parties from the perspective of the moral teachings of the Gospels.

> Political activities are no more exempt from moral accountability than any other form of human behaviour. Our task as Church leaders, therefore, is to share with you what the Gospels teach on justice in society.[7]

Principles

To this end, the *Statement of Intent* outlined five principles which, it urged, should guide the formulation of public policy: the dignity of every human being, the importance of community, the imperative of pursuing the common good, the centrality of work as an expression of human worth and self respect, and the requirement to give priority to the needs of the poor and the most vulnerable. In each case the principles were stated with brevity and little explanatory comment. It was acknowledged by the church leaders that there were other principles that were relevant for the pursuit of a just society, but these were not spelled out.

In closing, the church leaders acknowledged the 'sacrifice and commitment from those who serve our nation and communities', and urged their members not to be cynical or apathetic.

> The task which faces us all if we want a better, more human society, is to challenge policies which are in conflict with gospel vision and values. We look for policies that promote human dignity, stress human rights and responsibilities, emphasise the value of work and creativity, and express human compassion.[8]

The subsequent, and more detailed, *Social Justice Statement* was structured around the five principles outlined in the earlier document. It commenced with a brief discussion of the nature of social justice:

> The Churches cannot avoid confronting the requirements of social justice. The commitment to social justice is an essential part of life lived according to the Gospel of Jesus Christ and in response to the prophetic words found in other parts of the Bible. (§.2)
>
> Social justice is: fairness in our dealings with other people; fairness in the way responsibilities are shared; fairness in the distribution of incomes, wealth and power in our society; fairness in the social, economic and political structures we have created; fairness in the operation of those structures so that they enable all citizens to be active and productive participants in the life of society. (§.3)

Recognising the distinctive nature of New Zealand society, the *Statement* affirmed the Treaty of Waitangi and argued that 'a primary focus of our social justice concerns must be the special relationship which exists between Maori and all other New Zealanders' (§.7).

> The Treaty establishes a covenant relationship between Maori and the Crown and was born out of a concern for just relationships within this land. Though the Treaty has frequently been disregarded by law makers, Maori people have never forgotten it ... . If we are to have a just society in this land, the place of the Treaty and its potential to shape our future needs to be more widely acknowledged. (§§.7, 8)

The major part of the document (about 35 of the 51 paragraphs) deals with the 'principles which lie behind our concern for social justice' (§.6). As in the previous *Statement of Intent*, these were summarised as: 'to respect human dignity with its rights and responsibilities; to live in solidarity with others, aware of our interdependence; to seek the wellbeing of all; to value work and creativity; and to give priority to the needs of the poor' (§.6). The document discusses each principle in turn, seeking to explain its meaning, theological basis, and broad policy implications. At the conclusion of each of the five sections, the church leaders indicate very briefly the course of action they intend to urge upon the National government so as to give effect to the relevant principle.

An illustration of the methodology adopted by the authors can be gleaned from their treatment of two of the five principles: human dignity and giving priority to the needs of the poor. The latter principle was summarised in the *Statement* by the now common phrase, especially in Catholic circles, 'the preferential option for the poor'.

Human dignity, according to the *Statement*, is grounded in the 'conviction that all persons are created in the image of God and are to be valued unconditionally' (§.11). The *Statement* also appeals to the life and ministry of Jesus, highlighting the way he 'showed us that the essential dignity of every person is to be respected' (§.11). In order to protect this dignity, it is argued that individuals must be guaranteed certain rights, such as the 'right to food, housing, clothing, rest, education, health care, employment, and security in old age' (§.12). These rights carry with them 'corresponding responsibilities' for both individuals and the state. At the conclusion of the section on human dignity, the church leaders pledge that they will ask whichever political party is elected in the 1993 general election 'to review the adequacy of all benefits, and to explore with church and community social service organisations what new initiatives are required to meet people's needs' (§.17).

On the topic of 'the preferential option for the poor' the *Statement* observes, 'The way society responds to the needs of its poor through its public policies is the litmus test of how just or unjust a society it is, and how just or unjust its government' (§.41). The principle of giving priority to the needs of the poor is based on the fact that the 'poor and vulnerable have a special place in Christian teaching' (§.41). Surprisingly, the *Statement* provides few scriptural or theological justifications for this claim (despite the wealth of material available). It simply refers to Jesus' words as recorded in Matt. 25:40: 'Just as you did it to one of the least of these, you did it to me'. As it happens, the meaning and application of this text has been the subject of considerable scholarly debate. Arguably, Jesus is referring here to the 'least of the brethren', that is to say, those who have the greatest needs amongst the community of believers. If this is so, then the moral injunction in this instance is to serve the needy within the community of faith rather than the poor within the wider society. Consequently, it is open to debate whether this particular text should be used as a basis for guiding a nation's social policy (see Chapter 4).

The *Statement* emphasises that the poor include not merely those who are materially poor, but also those who are vulnerable (e.g. the psychiatrically disabled, the frail elderly, the defenceless unborn, etc.). If priority is to be given to the poor, then meeting their needs must be an 'integral element in economic and social policy rather than a hoped for by-product'. The *Statement* goes on to argue that the burden of 'economic restructuring has not been shared fairly' (§.45), that the demands of voluntary agencies 'have grown enormously' in recent years, and that poverty has become all 'too common' (§.43). Lamenting the 'tendency to project blame on to the needy as though they are the authors of their misfortune', it claims that most people are the 'unwilling victims of systems and policies which overlook their needs' (§.44). The relevant section of the *Statement* concludes by calling on the government to ensure that 'no citizen of our land experience a life deprived of life's essentials' (§.44), and seeking immediate political action to alleviate the 'plight of the poor' (§.46).

The principles embraced in the *Social Justice Statement*, especially the emphasis given to the needs of the poor and the broad endorsement of a market economy, are consistent with many similar documents prepared by church leaders and commissions during the past decade elsewhere in the world. For example, there are close parallels with such documents as: *Not Just for the Poor: Christian Perspectives on the Welfare State* (a report prepared in the mid-1980s by the Social Policy Committee of the Board for Social Responsibility of the Church of England); *Just Sharing: A Christian Approach to the Distribution of Wealth, Income and Benefits* (a report prepared in the late 1980s for the Church and Nation Committee of the General Assembly of the Church of Scotland); and *Economic Justice for All: Catholic Social Teaching and the U.S. Economy* (a pastoral letter prepared in the mid-1980s by the National Conference of Catholic Bishops in the United States). Admittedly, each of these documents is much longer and more comprehensive in its treatment of the issues than the *Social Justice Statement*. But the principles they espouse are remarkably similar. In this respect, New Zealand's church leaders can be said to be in step with the social theology embraced by their colleagues in many other countries, certainly those in advanced industrialised democracies.

The Role of the State

The church leaders advance an essentially positive view of the role of the state. Minimalist prescriptions are stoutly rejected. Their political theology is thus much closer to Catholic social teaching (see Chapter 5) than, say, conservative Reformed or Lutheran perspectives. Accordingly, the state's role is not simply to restrain evil and maintain law and order. Its aim should not be to do as little as possible, as if 'the government which governs least governs best' (§.28). On the contrary, the state has a much broader divine mandate:

> ... it bears ultimate responsibility for safeguarding the basic wellbeing of all. It is to act where private initiative does not suffice, by supporting the work of voluntary agencies. It is above all to choose policies which will truly serve the needs of the most needy among us. (§.44)

The church leaders explicitly reject both totalitarianism and 'the 'free market' approach which places human wellbeing at the mercy of economic forces alone' (§.29).

> New Zealanders have a range of convictions about the precise role of government. Some hold that its only role is to ensure the nation's security and to foster law and order. They argue for minimal government, that is government which does not intervene in areas such as health, housing, education and welfare, but leaves these to private enterprise and market forces. Others hold that government has a wider purpose. We are among them. For us, the purpose of government is to serve the common good, that is, to secure and protect the dignity of every citizen. Therefore government is to provide conditions where each is enabled to respect the rights of others, and where each can enjoy freedom and fulfilment in the economic, political and cultural life of the nation. (§.26)

From the perspective of the church leaders, the state has a major role to play in society. It must seek justice, protect human rights, ensure that basic needs are satisfied, and 'promote and preserve conditions within which human physical, mental and spiritual wellbeing may flourish' (§.13). Consistent with this, the leaders reject any suggestion that the state is an end in itself. Rather, its justification is instrumentalist in nature: 'It exists to serve its citizens according to the purposes of God' (§.45). The implication, then, is that if justice and the common good could be achieved without a state, there would be no need for such an organisation. The fact of the matter, however, is that they cannot. Hence, the state is a crucial and indispensable instrument in the quest for a just society.

While defending an active role for the state, the *Statement* acknowledges, albeit fleetingly, that the state 'cannot meet all human needs' (§.13). Likewise, it emphasises that the state should not seek to intervene unnecessarily in its pursuit of justice, and must uphold rather than undermine human freedom. In this respect, the *Statement* endorses two central principles, both drawn from Catholic social teaching. The first is the principle of subsidiarity (currently prominent in debates over the division of powers within the European Union). This principle maintains that the state should only undertake 'those activities which exceed the capacity of individuals or private groups acting independently' (§.27). The second, closely related, principle is that of supplementation. This 'requires that government assist communities and individuals to contribute more effectively to social wellbeing, and supplement their activity when the demands of justice exceed their capacities' (§.27).

Recommendations

The church leaders deliberately eschewed detailed policy recommendations in the *Social Justice Statement* preferring to concentrate on matters of principle. There were two main reasons for this. First, they wished to avoid the possibility of becoming embroiled in public debate over what might be regarded as 'technical' matters, such as the level of welfare benefits for particular categories of people, the structure of the tax system, or the form of means-testing. Precise policy prescriptions were believed to be the proper responsibility of those with expertise in the relevant fields. Second, from a strategic point of view they calculated that the *Statement* would be more influential politically if it avoided detailed policy recommendations, especially recommendations that were associated with a particular party. No doubt there was also a desire by some of the church leaders to minimise the possibility of alienating members of their churches and causing unnecessary internal divisions. More generally, the advocacy of broad principles rather than specific policies reflected the influence of a particular school of thinking about the proper the role of the church and theology in public affairs, namely the 'middle-axiom' approach. I will explore the nature and merits of this approach later in the chapter (see also Chapter 5).

Despite their concerns over the growth of poverty, the church leaders deliberately avoided recommending higher benefit levels or a more progressive tax system (even though most of them supported such measures). Instead, they emphasised the need for various policy reviews, specifically calling on the government to 'review the adequacy of all benefits' (§.17), review the 'equity of the present tax structure' (§.34), and 'promote new and resolute policies for the creation of full employment' (§.40). They also advocated a more consultative approach to policy-making, arguing that 'a more participatory democracy is desirable and possible' (§.23).

Responses to the *Social Justice Statement*

The absence of clear policy recommendations in the *Statement* drew sharp criticism. On the one hand the church leaders were criticised for their lack of conviction and for failing to provide adequate guidance to policy-makers. On the other hand many commentators interpreted the call for reviews of benefit levels and the tax system as evidence that the church leaders actually supported more generous benefits and higher taxes on the wealthy but were unwilling to say so publicly. They then attacked the leaders for not being more honest and direct, and for lacking integrity. Invariably, critics of a conservative or neo-liberal orientation also rejected the need for higher benefits or a more progressive tax system. Such responses highlight the difficulties which face church leaders in commenting on controversial social and political issues. In a sense, they are caught between a rock and a hard place. If they endorse concrete policy proposals, they expose themselves to accusations that they have strayed beyond their field of competence, that they have become too political, and, more simply, that they are wrong. If they fail to be specific, they can just as readily be accused of fudging the hard questions and of lacking the courage to take a stand. There is no simple solution to this conundrum.

As noted, with the exception of the main opposition parties, most of the responses by politicians, editorial writers and business groups to the *Social Justice Statement* were negative. Not merely were most commentators critical, but much of the criticism was harsh, disparaging and personalised. The church leaders were accused of being self-righteous, naive, woolly, ignorant, and out of touch with the views of their congregations. The *Statement*, likewise, was variously condemned for advancing a 'Utopian vision',[9] for being 'unremittingly negative and hopeless in its emphasis',[10] for its 'support for interventionist, essentially socialist philosophy',[11] for failing to 'confront hard policy issues',[12] for being 'unbalanced' and lacking 'rigorous political thought',[13] for advocating 'simplistic solutions',[14] and for 'courting a return to the borrow and tax days of the Muldoon era'.[15] The then Minister of Social Welfare, Jenny Shipley, although welcoming a debate on social justice, vigorously criticised both the *Social Justice Statement* and *Making Choices*. 'I am disturbed personally – and I say this as an active member of the church – that some of the work that has been put in front of this nation that purports to be the position of the church, in fact comes out of some of the most left-wing thinking areas of New Zealand'.[16]

Various policy advisers and economists with church connections were also dismayed by the *Statement*, believing it to be ill-conceived and unduly optimistic about the capacity of the state to rectify social and economic problems.[17] Such critics, however, appear to have given little attention to the more detailed analysis of various policy issues in *Making Choices*. In fact, *Making Choices* received virtually no media attention.[18] This was in spite of its wide distribution amongst journalists and policy-makers.

Among the few people of any prominence to lend public support to the church leaders was Professor Lloyd Geering of Victoria University. In an article published in *The Dominion*, Geering argued that the *Social Justice Statement* was by no means radical, let alone revolutionary. On the contrary, it was 'mild and almost timid'.[19] Moreover, many of the principles it enunciated were similar to those embraced in the statement issued by the Labour government's Economic Summit Conference in 1984. This statement, at the time, enjoyed the support of most key interest groups, including all the main business associations. Geering also pointed out that the church leaders were entirely justified in highlighting the growing problems of poverty, deprivation, and unemployment. It was beyond dispute that the burdens of economic restructuring had been unfairly shared: they had fallen primarily on the least advantaged members of the community.

But why did the church leaders generate such a hostile reception within the policy community and amongst opinion leaders? Why was the call for social justice apparently so unpopular? Why was there such a reluctance to admit the seriousness of the problems of poverty? And why was there an unwillingness to accept that the rapid growth of foodbanks since the early 1990s was a direct result of National's benefit cuts? One thing can be said with confidence: the negative responses were not primarily due to a belief that the church leaders, or the church in general, should stay out of politics. Most serious critics of the Statements, whether coming from an explicitly Christian standpoint or not, argued that it was thoroughly appropriate for the church to contribute to public debate.[20] There were few suggestions that political, economic and social policies were beyond the legitimate orbit of the churches or that it was improper for Christian leaders to comment on issues of justice and the common good.

Other explanations, therefore, must be sought for the unfavourable public response to the Social Justice Initiative. One reason almost certainly lies in the fact that since the mid-1980s New Zealand has been dominated by market-liberal rhetoric and a stridently anti-statist policy agenda. It has been a period in which macroeconomic stabilisation, economic liberalisation, privatisation, and the rolling back of the state have been the central concerns of policy-makers. In keeping with this, many of the social objectives and policies pursued by the state since the 1930s have been under increasing challenge. Notable here has been the reduced governmental commitment to redistributive policies and a diminished concern for the needs of the poor and marginalised. Against this background, the church leaders' Statements represented a challenge, albeit a relatively moderate, cautious, and tempered one, to the prevailing conservative, anti-welfarist ethos. By calling for more governmental action to alleviate poverty and curb unemployment, and by offering their tacit support for higher taxes, the Statements were out of sympathy with significant portions of business, political and editorial opinion. Had the Statements made an unequivocal call for less rather than more government, had they advocated less rather than the possibility of more taxes, they would doubtless have evoked a different response.

Second, and related to this, the Social Justice Initiative was a direct challenge to the policies and priorities of the National government. The church leaders' unambiguous comments about the gravity of the current social problems afflicting the community and the urgent need for key policy areas to be reviewed pointed to serious defects in the government's economic strategy. As such, the Social Justice Initiative was unavoidably political in character, all the more so given that 1993 was an election year. That the church leaders' Statements generated trenchant rebuttals from members and supporters of the government, therefore, is hardly surprising.

Last, at least some of the criticisms of the Statements were probably justified. Arguably, neither Statement was crafted with sufficient care or rigour. They were thus relatively easy targets for their critics. The *Social Justice Statement*, in particular, bears the hallmarks of indelicate phrasing and a lack of definitional clarity, especially with respect to key principles and concepts such as social justice and the common good. Social justice is defined as 'fairness', but the latter term is left undefined (see Chapters 2 and 3 for a more detailed analysis). Likewise, the meaning of the 'common good' is not specified. Whether and how social justice and the common good are related is also left unclear (see Chapter 5 for a discussion of this matter).

Vagueness is a problem in other parts of the *Statement*. Take, for example, the church leaders' views concerning the justifications for government intervention. Such intervention, they claim, 'is wholly justified when it helps other social groups contribute to the common good by directing, urging, restraining and regulating political and economic activity as circumstances require and necessity demands' (§.28). What precisely does this mean? How do we know when social groups are contributing to the common good (especially in the absence of a clear definition of the common good)? What does it mean to direct, urge, restrain or regulate 'political' activity? How do we determine 'when circumstances require and necessity demands'? What are the relevant criteria for evaluating the circumstances? What are necessities? If this lack of clarity were an isolated case, the complaints of the critics would have little justification. Regrettably, however, there are other examples of loose expression.

Among the many criticisms levelled at the *Social Justice Statement*, several deserve special mention. Despite the document's endorsement of the principle of subsidiarity, it places a heavy emphasis on collective (i.e. state) responsibility and collective solutions to economic and social problems. It also strongly criticises what it calls 'selfish individualism' (§.20) and gives considerable weight to the interdependence of humanity. A common theme amongst many of the critics was the view that the authors gave too little attention to the role of individual responsibility. The *Statement* maintains that 'most' of those who suffer misfortune, for example in the form of unemployment, 'are the unwilling victims of systems and policies which overlook their needs' (§.44). Although such claims may well be true, the *Statement* gives little recognition to the misfortunes which are largely the product of an individual's own doing. Likewise, it ignores the fact that a significant number of beneficiaries over the years have abused the system and secured state assistance for which they were not entitled.

Related to this, the *Statement* makes few references to the problems which can be generated by governmental action. State provision of social assistance can reduce the incentive for individuals to seek employment, thereby increasing dependency and reducing individual initiative. Social assistance programmes can also generate problems with respect to privacy and stigma, and exacerbate, as well as reduce, problems of injustice. Quite apart from this, raising tax revenue to fund income transfers and other social programmes imposes costs on the economy (including compliance and enforcement costs). These and other problems are largely ignored by the *Statement*. While rightly emphasising the importance of redistribution in the interests of social justice, the document gives only fleeting attention to the task of wealth creation. Admittedly, the section on 'work' acknowledges the responsibility for individuals to use their gifts and 'to contribute to the welfare of others' (§.36). But little is said about the need for economic growth or the creation of wealth. Nor does the document say much about the proper role of the state in ensuring that individuals have the appropriate incentives, as well as opportunities, to use their gifts to the full.

In short, the *Social Justice Statement*, despite its laudable objectives and commendable principles, contains some unfortunate defects. By attempting to cover a wide range of complex areas in a relatively short document, it almost inevitably fell into the traps of generality, imprecision, and banality. By seeking, correctly in my view, to emphasise the needs of the poor and the deficiencies of the existing policy regime, it failed to address the potential costs and drawbacks of alternative courses of state action. Finally, by largely ignoring the costs of, and limitations to, state action, it left its authors open to the allegation that their politics and social theology were unduly optimistic and insufficiently mindful of the dangers and drawbacks of a comprehensive welfare state. In short, it gave the impression, albeit unintended, that politics could provide solutions to most of the nation's social and economic ills. A greater emphasis on the limits of political action – on the fact that there is much which politics, no matter how well directed, cannot redeem or solve – would have been more consistent with some of the central tenets of the Christian faith.

The Contribution of Theology and the Church to Public Affairs

The Social Justice Initiative raises important questions about the way the church should seek to contribute to public affairs and influence public policy. One of these is whether the church and its leaders should make pronouncements on the merits of specific government policies or recommend particular policy initiatives. Directly related to this is the broader question of whether theology should be used as a basis for determining the details of public policy, or whether it should be confined to the more limited, but nonetheless vital, task of establishing the relevant ethical principles to guide policy-makers. Another issue is whether the church should set aside the language of theology and transcendence when it comments on important matters of public debate. Should it confine itself to the language of secular political discourse, or should it endeavour to shape the nature of this discourse by introducing theological categories? Quite apart from this, there is the issue of who should speak on behalf of the church in the realm of public affairs.

A common approach since the 1930s, particularly in Anglican circles, has been the view that the church should not concern itself with the relative merits of specific policies. It should not, in other words, be in the business of policy advocacy, for the advocacy of particular policies is invariably contentious and goes beyond the church's field of competence. Instead, its role should be, to quote Forrester, 'to lay down principles, both general principles of a more or less universal validity, and intermediate principles which are relevant and operational in a particular context'.[21] These intermediate principles have been referred to as 'middle axioms'; hence the so-called middle-axiom approach or method.

The middle-axiom approach was first advocated by J.H. Oldham in the 1930s. It was subsequently endorsed by various theologians with an interest in social and political ethics, perhaps the most notable being the Anglican Archbishop, William Temple.[22] A central feature of this approach is the contention that a Christian response to the issues of public policy should be a collaborative, interdisciplinary, and preferably ecumenical affair. More specifically, the aim should be to bring 'together groups of people with varied and relevant skill and experience to analyse the matter in hand, engage with the facts of the case, reflect theologically, and make recommendations'.[23] Such groups should include theologians as well as those with expert and practical knowledge of the issues in question, including if possible people with the responsibility for making decisions. In this way, the insights of theology can be brought to bear in the context of a full understanding of the complexities, constraints, and possibilities facing policy-makers. Similarly, theology can be 'earthed' by ensuring that the realities of the situation, be they political, scientific, economic or whatever, were properly taken into account. By virtue of this approach, it is argued, the utterances of the church, or its leaders, on important matters of public policy can avoid 'vacuous and high-flown generalities', while at the same time remaining free of unduly precise or misguided policy recommendations.[24]

Another central feature of the middle-axiom approach is a reliance on a deductive mode of reasoning. To quote Forrester:

> One starts by formulating what one might call pure theological truth; from this one elicits general principles of a universal nature; from these one derives middle axioms, or statements of the bearing of general principles in a particular context, providing a sense of direction; and finally (by the least clearly defined stage in the process) one chooses among the various policy options which might implement the middle axiom.[25]

From this perspective, then, middle axioms provide the link between general statements of principle, based on the ethical demands of the gospel, and the specific details of public policy. In the words of the World Council of Churches, middle axioms are 'those goals for society which are more specific than universal Christian principles and less specific than concrete institutions or programmes for action'.[26] Or, to quote Oldham and t'Hooft:

> They are an attempt to define the directions in which, in a particular state of society, Christian faith must express itself. They are not binding for all time, but are provisional definitions of the type of behaviour required of Christians at a given period and in given circumstances.[27]

An advocate of the middle-axiom approach might argue, by way of example, that a general principle might be the dignity of human beings; a related middle axiom might be that people should be treated fairly in the workplace; a specific policy to achieve this objective might be a legal code setting out certain minimum conditions of employment which must be observed in all workplaces. Such distinctions, however, are rather arbitrary, a point I will return to shortly.

Advocates of the middle-axiom approach maintain that while it is proper, indeed vital, for the church to formulate broad principles and middle axioms, it should leave it to those with the relevant expertise to translate such axioms into concrete policy proposals. Thus, the derivation of governmental programmes from middle axioms should be the task of individual Christians and policy-makers, not the church (whether this be its leaders, councils, or theologians). Technical matters should be left to those with the relevant technical experience. As Paul Ramsey has put it:

> Christian political ethics cannot say what should or must be done but only what may be done. It can only try to make sure that false doctrine does not unnecessarily trammel policy choices or preclude decisions which might better shape and govern events.[28]

Similarly, Archbishop Temple thought it was perfectly acceptable for church leaders, in their capacity as Christian citizens, to propose a certain course of action, but wrong for them to do so in their capacity as church leaders. Nor should the church, through its councils, assemblies or convocations, promote concrete policy initiatives or political programmes. As he put it: 'The Church is committed to the everlasting Gospel and to the Creeds which formulate it; it must never commit itself to an ephemeral programme of detailed action'.[29]

Yet, notwithstanding the intuitive appeal of the middle-axiom approach, it presents many difficulties.[30] To begin with, the approach assumes that it is possible for interdisciplinary and ecumenical groups to reach agreement on general ethical principles and the relevant middle axioms. Experience, however, demonstrates that this is frequently not the case. In fact, many church-based commissions and taskforces, both in New Zealand and elsewhere, have failed to come to a common mind on important social and political issues (e.g. the ethics of nuclear deterrence, the acceptability of homosexual lifestyles, the merits of *in vitro* fertilisation, etc.). Alternatively, agreement may be reached, but its price may be high: the principles and axioms arrived at may be vacuous and platitudinous, offering neither guidance nor inspiration.

Another questionable assumption underpinning the middle-axiom approach is the view that in seeking ethical guidance from the gospel, the church can derive principles and axioms that would be readily accepted by all people of good will, irrespective of their world view. Put differently, it is assumed that principles and axioms can be derived and expressed in the appropriate language of philosophical and political discourse such that they do not bring offence to those who reject the Christian faith. A broadly similar line of reasoning was advanced by Michael Irwin in his critique of the *Social Justice Statement*. In his view, when church leaders

> ... are addressing the community of faith they can invoke its sacred texts and traditions as well as reason for their arguments. If they are addressing the wider community, they need to appeal to reason and community values.[31]

There is clearly some merit in such a view. If the church wishes to communicate to the world and influence governmental policy, it must speak in a language that can be readily understood. The translation of the relevant theological categories and insights into contemporary parlance will thus be vital. Nevertheless, it is questionable whether appeals to the Scriptures and the specific doctrines of the church can or ought to be entirely eschewed in the public arena. It is equally questionable whether the church in its pronouncements on important matters of public policy can always avoid causing umbrage amongst those who reject a Christian world view.

A somewhat different but related assumption is that the distinctiveness and uniqueness of the Christian indicatives and imperatives can be filtered out and the truth translated into a more relevant, contemporary or rationalistic idiom. Such an approach has been aptly summarised by one of its leading critics Oliver O'Donovan:

> When the church contributes to public debate on matters of concern to society at large, it should forget that it is the church of Jesus Christ and should address society in terms common to all participants. The attempt to be distinctively Christian belongs only to the pursuit of internal discipline among the faithful.[32]

Such an approach, however, is open to various objections. Attempting to filter out the distinctive features of the Christian faith so that principles and axioms can be derived which are capable of winning the consent of reasonable people is by no means an easy or straightforward task. More important, if the Christian story, if the gospel, can in fact be filtered out, the question arises as to whether it is relevant and valid in the first place. Indeed, it suggests that the Christian faith is dispensable and that the business of formulating general principles and axioms to guide the formulation of public policy can proceed equally well, if not better, without the baggage of transcendence. Yet what is the point, one might ask, of the church simply affirming and reiterating what others have said, and doing so in exactly the same language? Surely, if Christians are to be faithful to the gospel, if they are to take their prophetic responsibility seriously, they have no choice but to emphasise the gospel's central features, its distinctive dogmatics as well as its distinctive ethics, no matter how disagreeable, or even offensive, some may find the message. If Christianity has something distinctive to say about human affairs, then the leaders of the churches ought, in the words of R.H. Tawney:

> ... whatever the cost, to state fearlessly and in unmistakable terms what precisely they conceive that distinctive contribution to be. If they do not, then let them cease reiterating secondhand platitudes, which ... bring Christianity into contempt.[33]

A further problem with the middle-axiom approach is the notion that the church ought not to comment on so-called technical matters; it should confine itself to matters of value, rather than matters of fact. Technical problems require technical analyses and solutions, not theological ones. Plainly, there are some inherent dangers with this approach. One is that it is possible to claim that many problems in society – unemployment, drug addiction, pollution, climatic change, traffic accidents, infertility, and so on – are primarily technical in nature. Accordingly, there is little role for the church or theology. In the face of such an argument, the church has only a few options: it can retreat to the increasingly narrow and increasingly irrelevant world of the non-technical;

it can question the designation of particular problems as 'technical'; or it can challenge the view that technical matters are beyond its proper ambit. In my view, it is the last of these options which the church should embrace. To do otherwise, is to concede that there are fields of human endeavour and forms of human conduct that are, in a sense, autonomous and thus exempt from legitimate theological scrutiny. It is to suggest that theology has little, if any, contribution to make to such disciplines as accounting, economics, law, medicine, or the biological and physical sciences. It is to suggest that the church must not offer public comment on 'technical' matters such as the merits of nuclear power, *in vitro* fertilisation, or strategies to relieve unemployment. Yet as Forrester has argued:

> ... the church must not allow itself to be intimidated by the suggestion that its judgements are invalidated by the largely technical nature of the problems: at every point ethical and religious considerations are interwoven with technical factors, and the church has a responsibility to judge and assess the issues at stake in the light of the gospel.[34]

Of course, in addressing matters of an arguably technical nature, the church and its spokespersons need to take particular care. They should in the first instance consult with those who have the relevant technical expertise and clarify the issues which are at stake. But they should not refrain from providing ethical guidance merely because there are technical considerations which need to be taken into account.

There are, however, even more serious problems with the middle-axiom approach. Central to the approach is the claim that it is possible to identify middle-level principles that fall somewhere between universal principles and specific directives or policy prescriptions. Yet this middle ground is potentially vast, and it is not at all clear where the boundary lines should be drawn between axioms and principles at the one extreme, or axioms and directives at the other. Take, for example, the area of taxation. Are the claims that 'taxes should be fair', or that 'taxes should be progressive', or that 'people should not pay more than 50 per cent of their income in tax' general principles, middle axioms or policies? Political parties are inclined to state in their manifestos that they support 'fair taxes', and to regard such pronouncements as policy statements. Similarly, suppose one were to claim, as many church leaders have done in recent decades, that the strategy of nuclear deterrence and the use of nuclear weapons are both morally unjustified. Whether this is a general principle or a middle axiom is by no means clear. But irrespective of the answer, the policy implications are plain enough: no country should possess, use or threaten to use nuclear weapons. So to suggest that the church should confine itself to the higher ground of principles and axioms and avoid matters of policy is, in many cases, an impossible assignment. Some principles necessarily entail certain courses of action and rule out others.

Even if the boundary between a policy and an axiom (or principle) could be more clearly delineated, the argument that the church should only address the latter is open to various objections. Is it really responsible or constructive to affirm specific principles or middle axioms without indicating how they should be applied in practice? Is it helpful or relevant to suggest, for example, that the tax system should be fair without providing some guidance as to what this means? In some ways it is easy to specify the broad social purposes, ends or objectives which should be served by public policy – the public interest, the common good, social justice, and so on. The harder and more important task is to give meaning to these objectives by engaging in the messy and complex business of assessing the means by which they can be achieved. If the church refuses to get its hands dirty by evaluating the relative merits of the policy options, if it shies away from so-called technical questions, if it is unwilling to take sides, if it focuses primarily on the generalities and ignores the particulars, the relevance of its contribution to public affairs is likely to be limited and its witness muted.

Quite apart from this, axioms and policies are intimately connected. To quote Forrester:

> ... principles and middle axioms cannot be understood, elucidated or assessed except in relation to the policies which might be used to implement them. Principles need to be tested, reconsidered and modified in the light of the experience of trying to make them operational.[35]

Hence, there is a good case for combining the advocacy of principles (or middle axioms) with an attempt to specify the policy implications of these principles, as difficult and controversial as this latter task can be. This is not to suggest that the church or its spokespersons should be in the business of advancing comprehensive policy programmes in a similar fashion to political parties. But it does mean that it should be willing to take the risk of committing itself to specific policies in particular situations.

In summary, the middle-axiom approach can be challenged on a number of fronts. It suffers significant definitional weakness. Its methodology is difficult, if not impossible, to apply. And its embrace by the church runs the risk of undermining both the distinctiveness and relevance of the Christian message.

It is not being suggested here that the authors of the *Social Justice Statement* slavishly followed the middle-axiom approach. In fact, in many important respects they did not. They made explicit references to Scripture. They did not eschew the theological basis of their principles. They did not avoid the language of transcendence. They did not seek to disguise the distinctiveness of their Christian presuppositions (although they did deliberately associate their pursuit of social justice with the efforts of 'all people of goodwill' [§.5]). Nor did they confine themselves solely to the enunciation and elucidation of general principles (or middle axioms). Nevertheless, the decision to avoid explicit policy advocacy is certainly in conformity with the middle-axiom approach. Whether the Social Justice Initiative would have carried more conviction had the church leaders given a firmer policy lead is difficult to say. It is, of course, possible that they would have been unable to agree amongst themselves on policy proposals in areas like social welfare, health care, unemployment or taxation.

For the future, it would be unfortunate if it became the normal practice for church leaders to avoid making unequivocal policy recommendations. It would also be regrettable if they merely criticised existing policies without offering positive alternatives. There is, to be sure, a certain safety in retreating to the high ground of principle. There are obvious dangers in endorsing particular policy proposals: it may generate controversy, alienate church members and invite allegations of partisanship. Yet the church's mission is not primarily to seek safety or court political approval. It is to proclaim the truth, and to do so regardless of the costs. At the same time, those who speak publicly on behalf of the church have a responsibility to be theologically alert and careful in their pronouncements. If church leaders, whether individually or collectively, offer comment on the merits of specific policy proposals, criticise the policy direction of a government, or advocate a particular course of action, they must do so only after adequate reflection on the theological issues at stake, as well as proper consultation with those who are deemed to have the appropriate policy expertise. Further, they must argue their case, whatever this may be, with conviction, cogency and clarity. And they must not avoid reference to the theological assumptions and principles from which their values and judgements are derived.

Conclusion

Without doubt, the church leaders' Social Justice Initiative ranks as one of the most remarkable episodes in the history of the Christian church in New Zealand. It brought together in an unprecedented fashion the leaders of all the major denominational groupings to address matters of acute public concern, namely the increasing problems of poverty, economic hardship and social distress. The ensuing *Statement of Intent* and the *Social Justice Statement* marked the first occasion when the nature of a just society had been seriously considered and then pronounced upon by the church leadership in a collective and ecumenical fashion. It was a bold and controversial move. Yet it was fully consistent with the mission and prophetic ministry of the church. By identifying themselves with the needs of the weak, vulnerable and marginalised, and seeking positive governmental action on their behalf, the church leaders bore testimony to some of the central ethical imperatives of the gospel. As Forrester correctly asserts:

> The Christian faith cannot avoid a responsibility for the public realm. Because it is committed to seeking first the Kingdom of God and his righteousness, it must stand for justice and for peace, it must speak for the poor and oppressed, and it must support, challenge and disturb the powerful.[36]

While both Statements attracted a good deal of criticism, at least some of which was justified, they are important documents and deserve close and careful scrutiny. In the following chapters, some of the central arguments and principles advanced, particularly in the *Social Justice Statement*, are explored and assessed. Subsequent chapters also examine some of the wider theological issues raised by the church leaders' pronouncements.

Notes

1. For various reasons New Zealand has had a strong ecumenical movement. The main ecumenical organisation is the Conference of Churches of Aotearoa New Zealand, and this embraces the Catholic Church as well as most Protestant denominations. Prior to the Church Leaders' *Social Justice Statement* there had been a joint statement by the heads of various churches on the Treaty of Waitangi in 1990. See Ann Wansbrough,

'Making a Difference: What Can the Australian Churches Learn from the New Zealand Heads of Churches 1993 Program', *Making Choices: Social Justice for Our Times*, Board for Social Responsibility, Uniting Church of Australia, NSW Synod, 1994, p. 5.

2. For an analysis of the National government's social policy changes in 1991 and their impact on poverty see Jonathan Boston and Paul Dalziel (eds) (1992), *The Decent Society? Essays in Response to National's Economic and Social Policies,* Auckland: Oxford University Press, esp. pp. 100-25; Richard Randerson (1992), *Hearts and Minds: A Place for People in a Market Economy,* Wellington: Social Responsibility Commission; Ruth Smithies and Helen Wilson (eds) (1993), *Making Choices: Social Justice for Our Times,* Wellington: GP Print, pp. 128-140; Adrian Whale (1993), 'Voluntary Welfare Provision in a Landscape of Change: The Emergence of Foodbanks in Auckland', Masters thesis, Department of Geography, University of Auckland.
3. For a brief account of the background to the church leaders' Social Justice Initiative, see Ruth Smithies and Helen Wilson (eds) (1993), *Making Choices,* pp. 2-7. See also Ann Wansbrough, 'Making a Difference', pp. 6-14.
4. Subsequently an eleventh church, the Congregational Church, joined the Initiative.
5. For a detailed analysis of the responses within the various churches and the wider community, see Ann Wansbrough, 'Making a Difference', pp. 15-22.
6. Ruth Smithies and Helen Wilson (eds) (1993), *Making Choices*, p. 10.
7. Ibid., p. 8.
8. Ibid., p. 10.
9. M. Searle (1993), 'The Just Society', *Stimulus*, 1/4, p. 42.
10. John Terris, 'Churches Turn Back the Clock', *The Dominion*, 13 August 1993.
11. Agnes-Mary Brooke, 'Muddled Thinking', *The Dominion,* 11 August 1993.
12. Simon Upton, 'Churches Step into Politics', *The Dominion,* 19 July 1993.
13. Editorial, 'Poor Pulpit Politics', *The New Zealand Herald,* 14 July 1993.
14. Editorial, 'Miracles Need to be Funded', *The Dominion*, 13 July 1993.
15. Editorial, 'A Clerical View of Social Justice', *The Evening Post,* 13 July 1993.
16. Quoted in *The Dominion,* 22 July 1993.
17. See, for example, Michael Irwin, 'Don't Confuse Gospel with Ideologies', *The Dominion,* 12 August 1993.
18. See Ann Wansbrough, 'Making a Difference', p. 18.
19. Lloyd Geering, 'Caesar's Things Belong to God, Too', *The Dominion,* 22 July 1993. See also Lloyd Geering, 'Churches Must Monitor Self-interest', *The Dominion,* 1 December 1992.
20. See Michael Irwin, 'Don't Confuse Gospel with Ideologies'; M. Searle, 'The Just Society', pp. 42-44.
21. Duncan Forrester, *Beliefs, Values and Policies: Conviction Politics in a Secular Age,* Oxford: Clarendon Press, 1989, p. 16.
22. See William Temple, *Christianity and Social Order,* London: SPCK, 1976.
23. Duncan Forrester, *Beliefs, Values and Policies*, p. 17.
24. Ibid., p. 17.
25. Ibid., p. 26.
26. Quoted in ibid., p. 23.
27. Quoted in ibid.

28. Quoted in ibid., pp. 25-26.
29. William Temple, *Christianity and Social Order,* p. 41.
30. Duncan Forrester, *Beliefs, Values and Policies*, pp. 26-35.
31. Michael Irwin, 'Don't Confuse Gospel with Ideology'.
32. Oliver O'Donovan, *Resurrection and Moral Order,* Leicester: IVP, 1986, p. 20. For a detailed critique of this position see Oliver O'Donovan, *Principles in the Public Realm: The Dilemma of Christian Moral Witness,* Oxford: Oxford University Press, 1984.
33. Quoted in Duncan Forrester, *Beliefs, Values and Policies*, p. 32.
34. Ibid., pp. 31-2. For a critique of the position that the church should not address so-called technical matters, see Michael Horsburgh, 'Should the Church be Involved in Politics?', Paper prepared for a conference on 'Churches and Social Justice', University of New England, Armidale, 17-19 September 1993, pp. 19-22.
35. Duncan Forrester, *Beliefs, Values and Policies*, p. 33.
36. Quoted in Michael Horsburgh, 'Should the Church be Involved in Politics?', p. 25.

[illegible]

Chapter 2

Law, Justice and the State

Alan Cameron

Introduction: The *Social Justice Statement*

This chapter responds to the *Social Justice Statement* by providing a critique of the central ideas of law, justice and the state on which the *Statement* is based.

The church leaders in their *Social Justice Statement* invited church members to consider the biblical teaching on social justice and in an election year urged them to challenge the policies of the government and political parties in the light of that teaching. The *Statement* begins by asserting that adherence to a Christian faith rooted in this biblical teaching involves a commitment to social justice on the part of the churches and their members (§.2). It states that because 'Christian faith is concerned about the whole of life and every facet of our life together in society' it is therefore the responsibility of Christians, 'to join with all people of goodwill in working for a society whose structures serve truly just ends'(§.5). Christian principles lying behind the concern for social justice are said to include:

- respect for human dignity
- living in solidarity with others
- seeking the wellbeing of all
- valuing work and creativity
- and giving priority to the needs of the poor (§.6).

A Christian concern to live out these principles and to work for social structures which promote them implies a central role for government. The *Statement* is, therefore, primarily concerned to address the responsibility of the state for promoting social justice.

The *Statement* has implications for the role of law. In calling upon the government to implement just social policies the *Statement* implies that laws ought to be passed which give effect to those policies. This chapter examines the role of law in the context of the *Statement*'s central theme of social justice.

Before embarking upon an examination of the *Statement*, a brief account will be given of the approach adopted in this chapter. This approach goes under the description of Philosophy of the Cosmonomic Idea (PCI).

Philosophy of the Cosmonomic Idea (PCI)

Chapter 1 pointed out that a major contribution to the ideas contained in the *Statement* was made by the Catholic Church. This is particularly evident in the *Statement*'s advocacy of a positive role for the state, and its reliance on the concept of the common good and the principles of subsidiarity and supplementation (§§. 26-27). Chapter 1 contrasted this view of the state's role with the 'conservative Reformed or Lutheran perspectives'. In common with the latter, PCI has its immediate historical roots in the Reformation. It arose out of a particular strain of Dutch neo-Calvinistic thought which emerged in the latter part of the nineteenth century.[1] However, the perspective which PCI proposes, and which this chapter adopts, regarding the role of law and state is closer to the Catholic position than to those conservative perspectives. Before the main subjects of this chapter are examined I propose to explain some of the central features of this perspective.

One reason for providing this background is the relative ignorance of PCI in both Christian and non-Christian circles, at least in this part of the world.[2] Another reason is that PCI challenges many commonly-held assumptions regarding the nature of religion and its relation to human thought and action. Finally, the theory of state and law accompanying this approach is based on a view of the nature of society and its structures which is distinctively different from prevailing conceptions of society.

A central tenet of PCI is the conviction that all of life is religion. By this is meant that nothing in human life – no human activity and no part of reality within which humankind functions – exists apart from a religious root. All human creatures in all their activities live out their lives on the basis of beliefs under the directing influence of some central religious motivating force or spirit. This view implies that human thought and knowledge of whatever kind is also religious and rests on religious beliefs.[3] It rejects the assumption which has come to be widely accepted amongst both Christians and non-Christians in Western society that the religious and the secular realms (which includes within it scientific and intellectual pursuits) are separate and ought to be kept apart.

The basis for rejecting this limiting view of religion by PCI is found in the biblical themes of the 'Lordship of Christ'[4] and the 'Kingdom of God'[5] the religious implications of which are taken to be all-encompassing in relation to human life and society. Herman Dooyeweerd and D.T.H. Vollenhoven were the founders of the philosophical movement based on this fundamental tenet concerning the nature and role of religion. However, it is in the former's work that we find the development of ideas directly relevant to the subject of this chapter.

Dooyeweerd's systematic philosophy[6] challenged the presupposition of Western intellectual traditions concerning the 'autonomy of theoretical thought' by undertaking an investigation into the structure of theoretical thinking in order to reveal its religious roots.[7] He defined religion as an 'innate impulse of the human selfhood [ego] to direct itself toward the *true* or toward a *pretended* absolute Origin' of all temporal reality.[8] This innate impulse is focused on the religious centre of the human self, the human 'heart' which transcends temporal human existence.[9] Because all of a person's temporal functions concentrate on this religious centre of individual human existence, all of these functions express this religious nature. Human thinking, therefore, is an activity which at its deepest level is religious. It will always rest on religious assumptions or beliefs. Working from this conception of religion, Roy Clouser defines religious belief as 'a belief in something(s) or other as divine' or 'a belief concerning how humans come to stand in proper relation to the divine'. And he defines 'divine' as 'having the status of not depending on anything else'.[10]

By a 'transcendental'[11] critique of the history of Western thought, Dooyeweerd sought to lay bare the religious motivating spirits (or 'ground-motives') which directed the Western intellectual traditions and the religious beliefs on which they rested. According to this critique the major Western traditions comprised four major ground-motives. First, there is classical Greek thought, driven by the religious ground-motive of matter and form. The mediaeval-scholastic tradition was guided by the second ground-motive of nature and grace. The humanistic tradition, which broke radically with the scholastic tradition, is guided by the third ground-motive of nature (science) and freedom.[12] These ground-motives are religious, according to PCI, because they are the deepest spiritual roots which give direction to the major intellectual traditions and culture to which they belong.

Beside these three major religious motives Dooyeweerd posited a fourth ground-motive which he described as the biblical ground-motive of creation, fall and redemption.[13] This ground-motive was to provide the religious direction for a radically Christian reformation of theoretical thought and culture. Whilst not laying claim to infallibility or to some kind or theological purity, PCI bases its claim to being radically Christian on its conscious endeavour to be directed by the Christian ground-motive alone, eschewing any attempt to accommodate or effect a synthesis with other ground-motives.

Dooyeweerd's major work, *A New Critique of Theoretical Thought,*[14] was to be one of the first contributions to this intellectual reformation. He argued that theorising guided by the biblical religious motive required rejection of all attempts to accommodate non-Christian religious motives with the Christian religious motive. The scholastic schema of nature and grace, comprising a synthesis of the biblical motive with the Greek Form/Matter motive, was regarded by him as one such attempt. Mainstream Catholic thought, notably Thomism, was founded in this synthesis of Christian theology and Aristotelian philosophy. Dooyeweerd rejected such attempted syntheses. He considered the Christian and non-Christian religious motives to be fundamentally antithetical, only able to exist in a tension in which one or other of the two motives would eventually gain the ascendancy.[15] The idea of a fundamental religious antithesis in human thought is based on the biblical teaching addressed to both individuals and communities that it is not possible to serve two masters (Matt. 6:24). Given PCI's all-encompassing interpretation of religion , the injunction against serving two masters is as applicable to human thinking as to anything else in human life. The significance of Dooyeweerd's assessment of the Thomistic tradition will become apparent when the Catholic contribution to the *Statement* is examined.

Dooyeweerd's critique explained the religious ground-motives of Greek and humanistic thought as possessing a radical inner tension resulting from their dualistic structures. The root of modern humanistic thought was said to be the motive of freedom expressed in the idea of freedom of the person.[16] In its deepest religious sense this idea of freedom means freedom from any non-human (divine) ordering, freedom to exploit the resources of the earth and to utilise fully human capabilities for creating structures according to humankind's own design. An unfettered freedom to master and exploit the world's resources leads inevitably to the nature (science) pole of the freedom-nature motive coming to the fore. According to Dooyeweerd, an inevitable consequence of nature becoming dominant is that human freedom itself becomes threatened. Not only the natural world but the human creature also becomes subject to scientific/technical control.[17] Hence, within the humanistic ground-motive there exists a polar tension arising from its dualistic nature. The idea of human freedom features, for example, in the individualistic stream of political liberalism, including rational choice theory, which has come to predominate in economics and political science. Yet, often accompanying these forms of liberal theory is an excessive faith in the power of science and technology with potential for intrusive control at the expense of human freedom.[18] Dooyeweerd was able to show how the 'ideal' of science came to dominate in Western liberal theory. For example, under its influence, Thomas Hobbes produced a mathematical-mechanistic construction of society. His theories of natural law, state and human nature were strongly influenced by this pole of the humanistic religious motive.[19]

Dooyeweerd's transcendental critique of theoretical thought provided him with an explanation for the fundamental tension at the root of humanistic thought. He argued that any religious standpoint which locates the source of all being in anything other than the true transcendent origin (i.e. the God of Scriptures) must necessarily take its point of departure from within the creation. Such a starting point can only serve as a substitute for the true transcendent source of all creaturely existence and meaning. This insight was based upon an interpretation of the biblical idea of idolatry. Idolatry in this interpretation occurs whenever an attempt is made to replace the worship and service of the true origin of all creaturely existence (God) with a creaturely substitute (idol).[20]

From this idea of the religious character of all human existence, Dooyeweerd argued that human thought which rejects the divine origin as the source of its own activity must find a creaturely substitute as its religious root.[21] In so doing it must take its point of departure within creaturely existence, the so-called 'immanence' standpoint.[22] The latter, on this view, encompasses early Greek metaphysical theory and modern humanistic theorising. Dooyeweerd's critique set out to show that the immanence standpoint rested on a dogmatic belief in the autonomy or self-sufficiency of human thought (reason), the dogma that theoretical thinking is its own starting point.[23] Employing his idea of religion examined above, Dooyeweerd maintained that belief in the autonomy of human thought obscures the religious motives underlying that central belief by its very denial of the religious character of human thinking.[24]

Theory, Philosophy and World-Views

PCI self-consciously bases itself upon certain ideas concerning the nature of theory, the role of philosophy, and their relation to the idea of a Christian perspective or world-view. Dooyeweerd's critique set out to challenge both the so-called 'secular' traditions of thought and Christian intellectual traditions. Regarding the former, it did this by attempting to expose the religious character of all theorising and by redefining the function of theory and of philosophy in particular. With respect to the latter, it challenged the view that a systematically reasoned Christian approach to any subject comprises a theology of some description. The 'theological' approach is criticised because it often involves superimposing Christian assumptions upon existing secular theory. This approach is considered to be deficient by PCI in two main respects.

First, it fails to discern the non-rational, religious roots of the 'secular' philosophy on which it has to rely. It thereby fails to appreciate the extent to which secular philosophy may be incompatible with a Christian perspective. Second, the theological approach fails to appreciate the respective roles of theology and philosophy.[25] It is acknowledged that in many cases where the term 'theology' or 'theological' is employed, as for instance, in the phrases 'theology of work', or 'theology of justice' there is a genuine attempt being made to articulate a biblical perspective on the topic in question. In such cases the objection is not to the approach adopted but the inappropriate use of the term. Such usage, in the view of PCI, fails to recognise clearly the limited nature of theology as a special theoretical discipline amongst other disciplines. Clearly, however, this is a much less fundamental criticism than that made above in respect of the approach which attempts to superimpose a theology upon prevailing theories whatever the subject happens to be.

The task ascribed to philosophy implies that theology, as a special theoretical discipline, necessarily proceeds upon the basis of *philosophical* assumptions. Whilst this approach aims to deny to theology pre-eminence amongst the theoretical disciplines, including philosophy, it is not intended to substitute philosophy for theology as the main source of Christian truth. It is a fundamental tenet of PCI that the philosophical assumptions employed as the basis for Christian theorising should be shaped by a biblical world-view. The latter only presents itself to those who seek under the guidance of the Holy Spirit to discern and respond to the revelation of God's Word in the Scriptures of the Old and New Testament, in the person of Christ, and in the creation as a whole.[26] This idea of revelation implies that a Christian perspective on any matter arises not merely from a personal 'commitment to Christ' and devotion to the reading of the Bible, indispensable though these may be, but also requires insight into all of created reality, albeit, guided by a personal commitment and biblical insight.[27] When Christians, therefore, seek theoretical insight into issues of law, state and justice their theorising should be shaped by this biblical world-view.

Underlying the perspective presented in this chapter is a concern, by authors of the *Statement*, that the biblical principles of justice should be followed in the contemporary political and social life of our country. A political and legal theory informed by a biblical/religious world-view can play an important role in assisting this goal. PCI is a fallible human attempt to provide this theoretical assistance. The chapter now examines the specific contribution of this philosophy to a theory of society and to the subjects of law, justice and the state, with particular reference to the *Social Justice Statement*.

The Contribution of PCI to a Theory of Society

Dooyeweerd's critique of the Western tradition of theoretical thought was intended to clear the way for developing a Christian philosophy based on the biblical ground-motive of creation, fall and redemption. This philosophy took for itself the description Philosophy of the Cosmonomic Idea on account of the critical role it assigned to the notion of a ground-idea or cosmonomic idea.[28] Dooyeweerd maintained that for each of the basic ground-motives theoretical thought expresses itself in a corresponding ground-idea. Each ground-idea presupposes answers to three fundamental and indissolubly connected questions concerning the coherence, totality and origin of the cosmos, the last being the ultimate and most fundamental question.[29] These are transcendental problems, that is to say, they arise in the process of critical theoretical reflection, but, on account of their religious character, transcend theoretical thought.[30]

The ground-idea is not merely cosmic, informing a theoretical view of the entire cosmos, but '*cosmonomic*'. Dooyeweerd maintained that giving answers to the three transcendental problems of coherence, totality and origin implies the notion of a cosmic ordering or law, the classical Greek term for which is 'nomos'.[31] Hence, the Philosophy of the *Cosmonomic* Idea. The idea of a cosmic law is an interpretation of the biblical idea of 'the Word of God' understood as a law for humankind and the creation in which it is placed.[32]

According to Dooyeweerd, theoretical thought under the direction of the biblical religious ground-motive of creation, fall (into sin) and redemption is guided by a cosmonomic idea[33] which provides answers to the three problems concerning the origin, totality (or unity) and coherence of cosmic reality.[34]

The origin of reality and the starting point for theorising is God the Creator. The unity within the diversity of all reality is found in the 'lawful' requirement of love and service of God and fellow creatures. It is expressed within human experience in the person of Jesus Christ, the new religious root of the human race. The problem of coherence involves a question concerning the mutual relation between the 'modal aspects' of reality. The answer to this question is that each of the aspects is mutually irreducible (sovereign in its own modal sphere) but related to the other in an indissoluble coherence in the cosmic order of time.[35] An explanation of this theory of the modal aspects will shortly be given.

The theory of the modal aspects is a key element in Dooyeweerd's systematic philosophy both with respect to his ontology (theory of the nature of things, processes, social structures, etc.) and his epistemology (theory of knowing). His account of theoretical knowing is based upon an ontology of the theoretical act of thinking in which the theory of the modal aspects plays a critical role.[36] Dooyeweerd maintained that in the *ground-idea* of any theoretical account of reality is presupposed an account of the modal diversity of reality, of the diverse ways (modes) in which reality functions. His theoretical account of the structures of reality, both 'thing' structures (plants, stones, trees, etc.) and human structures (including the human person him/herself) builds upon the theory of modal aspects or spheres. Whilst aspects of the theory have been challenged and criticised,[37] the theory itself continues to play a central role for adherents of PCI.

Although Dooyeweerd's most influential and best known theoretical writing is his general philosophical work, *A New Critique of Theoretical Thought,* his main discipline was law. For many years he occupied the chair in jurisprudence at the Free University of Amsterdam. Philosophical problems which confronted him in legal and political thought provided the stimulus to develop the general systematics.[38] He applied his philosophical insights to jurisprudence,[39] philosophy of law,[40] sociology of law,[41] and to a theory of the state.[42]

A feature of Dooyeweerd's philosophy of law and state is the distinctive manner in which he conceives of the relationship between law and the state. This distinctiveness is owing to his theory of the modal aspects and the manner in which they express themselves in human structures. The following, therefore, will sketch his theory of the modal aspects and social structures, before examining PCI theory of state and law.

The Theory of the Modal Aspects

Dooyeweerd maintained that our everyday, primary ('naive') experience is of concrete things, processes, events and structures. *Theoretical* reflection upon that experience reveals that reality functions in diverse ways, or modes. These modes are distinct, irreducible aspects of experienced reality. Only in the analytical distinguishing of our thinking do the aspects present themselves as distinct modes. In our everyday experience of concrete things and processes, these aspects, though functioning in that concrete reality, are only implicit. Theoretical thought has the task of deepening our understanding of reality by reflecting on, and bringing explicitly to view, the modal character of that experience. Theory has the task of providing an explanation of *how* we experience things and processes as different kinds of things and processes.[43] It explains why things, processes and structures are experienced as economic, legal, social, historical, biological, or physical things, processes, and structures.

Within the 15 distinct modal aspects which Dooyeweerd discerned in the structure of human experience, he made a distinction between *normative* and *non-normative* aspects.[44] The aspects which qualify physical and biological phenomena are non-normative in the sense that the things themselves have no choice as to whether they obey the modal 'laws' which govern their existence. A thing such as a tree or a stone he characterised as functioning as a *subject* (actively) in the non-normative aspects only, although it functions as an *object* (passively) in all other aspects in which it does not function as subject, including all the normative aspects.[45] The last aspect in which the thing functions subjectively[46] is the *qualifying* or *leading* aspect of that thing. Hence, a stone is qualified as a physical thing. A tree is a biological thing because the biotic aspect is the last modal aspect in which the tree functions as a subject. Of course, it also functions in 'lower' aspects such as the physical.

Human structures,[47] however, are distinguishable from such natural phenomena. The modal aspects in which humans and their social structures function include all of the *normative* modal aspects. These modes of existence call forth a subjective normative response to the ordering which governs those aspects. Human structures,[48] such as the family, marriage, a voluntary society, a business organisation, and the state function in the normative aspects,[49] one of which will qualify, or characterise, that structure as the type of structure that it is. Hence, a business enterprise is an economic structure *qualified* by the economic mode. Similarly, the family and the marital bond are ethical or moral structures because they are qualified by the moral aspect in which the bond of love plays a leading role.[50] Whilst all human structures function in a diversity of normative aspects – social, ethical, legal, etc. only one of those normative aspects *qualifies* the whole structure and the other normative aspects functioning within it. For example, a business enterprise, no doubt, has an ethical dimension – loyalty and honesty are expected of both those in positions of authority, the officers, and the employees of the company. Such virtues are needed for the healthy functioning of the enterprise. Nevertheless, it is the economic aspect or functioning of the enterprise which colours or qualifies the whole structure, including its ethical dimension. The modal qualification in the structures (or 'structural principles') of the different social spheres gives to each their inviolable integrity, that ensures each is, normatively speaking, sovereign in its own sphere. The biblical basis of this principle of sphere sovereignty lies in the idea that God created everything according to its own nature'.[51] The relevance of this principle to some of the key ideas behind the *Social Justice Statement* will be explained later in the chapter.

Within each of the structures of society, human beings may subjectively respond to the normative ordering of each structure in either a positive or negative manner. Hence, within the family, parents may respond to the normative requirements of love towards their children in a better or worse way. Moreover, it is this duty of parental love and care – the ethical/moral aspect – which characterises the family relationship and the leading role of parents within this societal structure.[52] The marital relationship and other enduring, intimate relationships between persons are similarly qualified by the ethical normative aspect expressed in the form of mutual respect, trustworthiness and openness.

Values and Norms

It important to understand clearly what is entailed by PCI's conception of modal normative aspects functioning in human structures.[53] As part of God's law-like ordering for the creation, their existence does not depend on human subjective activity. In this sense they are not mere human 'values'. Nevertheless, God-given norms, for example, justice, love, economy, etc. require human response (positivisation) for their factual realisation in human experience. These norms apply to human life and in that sense 'exist'. But their existence is no guarantee of human obedience to them. God's creatures ought to respond to these norms by obediently positivising them within the structures of human society. Only in this sense do the norms become *human* values.

This conception of values or norms breaks fundamentally with the humanistic tradition of modern thought and its understanding of the relationship between facts and values. It implies a different interpretation of the distinctions between description and prescription, and between descriptive analysis and normative theory, which presuppose the commonly accepted interpretation of the fact-value distinction. One of the historically dominant traditions of legal theory, legal positivism, has been based on this fact-value distinction. Facts are in the realm of the observable or scientifically analysable. Values, on the other hand, are part of pure human subjectivity, mere human creations. But even legal positivism, at least in one version, now recognises that legal norms have factual existence and that actually existing legal institutions possess a normative character.[54] For example a contract, the legal form of marriage or a legal corporation are normative institutions which embody legal values or norms. In both the PCI view and this version of legal positivism, facts and values, 'is' and 'ought', are not mutually exclusive categories. An 'ought', that is a norm, is no less an 'is' or fact, albeit a different kind of fact than a physical thing or phenomenon.

Where PCI still fundamentally departs from legal positivism, of even the revised type, is in maintaining the view that positivised human norms presuppose the existence of God-given norms or principles. These norms are part of the divine 'law' or ordering for the creation. The formation of human norms in law, legal relations and institutions, or in ethical relations and institutions, are but subjective responses to the God-given law-ordering. These responses realise that normative ordering in human affairs. It is this divine, creational normativity to which the theory of the normative modal aspects refers.

The Theory of the State

Having introduced the theory of modal aspects and its application to human structures, and having also clarified the sense of 'normative' as applied to the modal aspects, the implications of this modal theory for a Christian theory of the state and law will now be considered.

In PCI the leading or qualifying function of the state is the juridical or 'justitial' modal aspect.[55] The juridical modal qualification of the state implies a normative requirement to do justice in a legal manner, in compliance with the norm of public justice.[56] The juridically qualified nature of the state is expressed, for example, in the doctrine of the rule of law, a fundamental doctrine in legal systems such as that of New Zealand, which belong to the Westminster tradition of constitutional law.[57]

Although Dooyeweerd characterised the state as having a juridical/legal qualification, the state is not the only structure or human process in which the juridical aspect functions. This is explained by one of the key elements of the modal theory. The latter holds that all modal aspects, including the juridical, function in some manner or other in *all* things, structures, and processes experienced within reality.[58] Dooyeweerd maintained that a private association, for example, a sports club, through its internal rules gives expression to the functioning of the juridical aspect within its structure. Even a family has its own informal legal rules (e.g. when meals will be served, when children may watch television) which may entail sanctions for their breach. But, it is only the state which is *qualified* by the functioning of the juridical aspect. Similarly the moral bond of love qualifies the human structures of family and marriage and enduring, intimate human relationships. Yet, the ethical aspect functions in all human relationships, including the state.

The manner in which non-juridical aspects function within the state, however, are governed by the leading or qualifying role which the juridical aspect plays. As a normative mode of reality the meaning of the juridical aspect is found, according to Dooyeweerd in the idea of retribution. However, retribution is not confined to its narrow penal sense. Instead, it is to be understood in the broad sense of a 'well-balanced harmonisation of a multiplicity of interests, warding off any excessive actualising of special concerns detrimental to others'.[59] This broad meaning is apparent in Dooyeweerd's characterising the leading juridical function of the state as one of *public justice*. For this reason I agree with Piet van Niekerk's suggestion that the modal meaning of the juridical aspect is captured in the idea of justice.[60] Roy Clouser's term 'justitial', therefore, is an apt description of this aspect.[61]

The Legal Theory of PCI and Other Theories of Law

The theory of law and state propounded by the adherents of PCI has been consciously set over against prevailing 'secular' or 'humanistic' theories. As we have seen, the Christian theory attributes to law and state a (divinely-sourced) normative character which other theories lack. An example of the latter is legal positivism which, until relatively recently, has been the view of the dominant school of legal theory in the Anglo-American tradition.[62] Legal positivism has maintained that morality (which includes justice) is not an intrinsic feature of human law. Law in this view has been characterised as an emanation of human power (e.g. Hobbes, Austin) or a system of rules which has no necessary connection with norms of justice or morality (e.g. H.L.A. Hart). Legality in this approach is largely a matter of convention dependent on the acceptance of a rule or criterion of formal legal validity.[63] The content of law may include morality but this content is contingent on the accepted practices and customs of the society.

Legal positivism has come under attack from various directions. Ronald Dworkin's ideas originate in the same liberal political tradition with which modern legal positivism is associated. Dworkin has criticised the positivist preoccupation with law as rules. He has emphasised the role of legal principles as embodying rights. Judges, he argues, must have resort to principles (integrity, equality, justice) which are grounded in the background morality of the political and legal institutions.[64]

Critical Legal Studies (CLS)[65] and postmodern legal theory[66] in general, attack legal positivism and Dworkinian liberal theory for failing to account for the indeterminacy and incoherency of law and for masking the ideological character of both law and legal theory.[67] Legal feminism has drawn upon these 'radical' theories in order to critique the gender bias in law.[68]

Such theories, with their claims of ideological bias in law and legal theory, have some striking similarities to the religious critique of modern legal and political culture found in PCI.[69] The latter, however, fundamentally departs from such theories in its biblically-inspired conviction that human law and legal structures are constrained by a divine normative ordering. Legal positivism and Dworkinian legal theory on the other hand, also possess features shared with the Christian legal and political theory. For example, the efforts of legal positivism towards providing an empirical analysis of law and its concepts have been matched by a complex analysis of legal concepts in the legal theory of Dooyeweerd and his successors.[70] PCI's legal philosophy also provides, in common with Dworkin, an important role for legal principles and rights.[71]

From the standpoint of PCI's legal theory, the most fundamental criticism of Dworkin and the legal positivists would be that they lack an explanation of the 'transcendental' normative basis of empirical (positivised) legal rules and norms (legal positivism), and principles (Dworkin). The transcendental normative basis of legal rules, norms and principles refers to the divine law-like ordering for the creation. According to PCI, positive law not only presupposes a human act of positivisation, but the concept of positive law or legal positivisation itself also presupposes a norm which is positivised in some legal form or other. For Dworkin and the legal positivists, the positivised norms are human values, the free creation of human subjectivity. The Christian philosophy's critique, however, contends that these 'secular' theories, cannot give a satisfactorily coherent account of law's normative character without presupposing some non-human (non-positive) normative source.[72] The non-human source, of course, is found in the divine normative ordering of creation. This ordering, whilst concretely expressed in human experience through human responses to it in the form of legal acts of positivising (e.g. law-making), at the same time transcends human experience and knowledge on account of its divine origin. This is what is meant by the divine norms of justice (or love, economy, etc.) being *transcendental.*

Thomist Theory of Law, Justice, State and Society

Legal positivism has traditionally been associated with a rejection of natural law theorising. One version of natural law theory, which originated in the mediaeval scholastic philosophy of Thomas Aquinas, is of particular relevance to the subject of this chapter. Elements of the Thomist natural law theory appear as part of the Catholic contribution to the *Social Justice Statement,* especially in that part (§§.26-34) dealing with the role of the state and its laws. A synthesis of Aristotelian philosophy and Christian theology, Thomistic natural law theory maintains that human law is supposed to conform to a higher natural moral law accessible to human reason. Natural law itself is 'the participation of the eternal [divine] law … in the rational creature'.[73]

PCI offers a different critique of natural law theory from that of legal positivism. Indeed, from a positivist standpoint, PCI might appear to be another version of natural law. PCI, however, distinguishes its idea of cosmic law or ordering from the idea of natural law, whether of the scholastic-mediaeval (Thomism), or humanist versions (Locke, Hobbes, Pufendorf, etc.). A major point of difference is that PCI wishes to avoid what it considers to be the pervasive rationalism of those theories. The place of human reason will be addressed below in the following examination of the Thomistic natural law influence on the *Social Justice Statement.*

The various conceptions of natural law are differentiated by PCI according to the religious ground-motives controlling those conceptions.[74] The Thomist version is explained as being under the directing of the motive of nature and grace, itself an attempted synthesis of Greek matter-and-form motive with the

Christian biblical motive. The influence of the Greek motive is seen to be expressed in the Thomist conception of human nature and human society.

Thomist philosophy views the human person as a dualism of a material body (matter) and a rational soul (form). In the natural realm the individual realises his or her nature in human communities of which the state is the highest and most complete expression.

> Thus for Thomas a social inclination or a predisposition toward society is also innate in rational human nature. This social propensity develops in stages, through the formation of smaller and larger communities that are mutually related in terms of *lower* to *higher*, *means* to *end*, *part* to *whole*.[75]

The state is the highest community to which all lower communities relate as parts to the whole. This conception of society with the state as its highest expression is derived from the Aristotelian teleological conception of society. In both Aristotle and Aquinas '[t]he state is based on the rational disposition of human nature. Its essence is *characterised* by its *goal*, the common good', which is 'the immediate basis of governmental authority'.[76]

Thomist and PCI Theories of State and Society Compared

There are at least three features of the Thomist account of human society which are shared with PCI. The first of these is anti-totalitarianism. Because Thomism conceives of the state as constructed from below, the lower communities possess a degree of autonomy over against the higher political community. For this reason Thomism is seen to be anti-centralist or anti-totalitarian in an absolutist sense.[77] The principle of subsidiarity adopted in Catholic teaching under the influence of Thomism is an expression of this anti-centralist conception.[78] This principle has assumed considerable importance in the context of the European Union, with implications for questions of sovereignty affecting states within the Union.[79] In the context of Thomistic thought, Dooyeweerd interprets the principle as follows:

> The rational law of nature holds that man depends on the community only for those needs which he himself cannot fill as an individual. The same natural law also holds that a lower community like the family or the school depends on the higher communities (ultimately on the state) only for those interests that it itself cannot handle.[80]

The principle of subsidiarity bears a strong resemblance to the principle of sphere sovereignty in PCI. Chaplin identifies three 'striking' similarities of substance. Both (i) repudiate individualistic social theories, (ii) develop pluralistic conceptions of society, and (iii) conceive of the state as having special responsibility for recognising and protecting a plurality of qualitatively different communities and for preserving harmony amongst them. This responsibility also requires vigilance against domination of any community, including the state itself, over other communities.[81]

A second feature shared by Thomism and PCI concerns the source of political authority. Both approaches hold to the biblical view of a divine source for the state's authority.

A third point of similarity relates to the distinctive nature of the state and its role. In PCI the state's structural principle is qualified by the norm of public justice. This characterisation of the leading function of the state bears a degree of similarity to the idea of the common good which is supposed to be the end, or goal (telos), of the state in the Thomistic conception of law and the state. The principle of subsidiarity provides a means by which the common good can be attained.

Notwithstanding these similarities, PCI insists that there are some important differences between itself and Thomism. Furthermore, these differences can be illustrated with reference to the similarities just considered.

First, the principle of sphere sovereignty requires a 'precise account of the intrinsic nature of the life spheres'.[82] The term 'sphere sovereignty' was first coined by Guilliame Groen van Prinsterer, a Dutch historian.[83] It received its 'classic formulation' in the work of Abraham Kuyper, a theologian, church leader and politician who became Prime Minister in the Netherlands from 1901-1905.[84] Dooyweerd developed the principle in a much more systematic fashion by applying his theory of the modal aspects to human structures. No one sphere, according to this principle, can become part of a larger whole.

The essentially Aristotelian conception of society out of which the principle of subsidiarity arises tends to view the state as a higher type of human community encompassing lower communities as its parts.[85] Thomism only distinguishes different communities according to their purpose (telos) and not their inner nature. Dooyeweerd thought that this lack of insight into the intrinsic nature of the different communal spheres of life resulted in the principle of subsidiarity with its assumption of higher and lower communities being unable to provide protection against political totalitarianism.[86] However, Chaplin has argued that this difference has been overstated and that Dooyeweerd himself incorporates an idea of an end or 'destination' in his account of human communities. Nevertheless, both reject the hierarchical view of society adopted by Thomism and implicit in the Catholic ideas of common good and subsidiarity.[87] Rather than rejecting the principle of subsidiarity itself, Chaplin rejects its hierarchical interpretation by incorporating it into Dooyeweerd's 'horizontal' view of the relations between qualitatively different communal spheres. In this approach the principle does not run in one direction only from the state as highest in the hierarchy. All communities lack self-sufficiency including the state, and all communities perform subsidiary functions with respect to all the others, again including the state. The state's lack of self-sufficiency is illustrated by its need to obtain taxes from corporations.[88] It can plausibly be argued that the existence of a state system able to provide assistance for the healthy functioning of other social spheres is dependent on well-developed economic and other non-state social structures. Through this reinterpretation of the principle of subsidiarity, Chaplin is able to meet Dooyeweerd's criticism of the Thomistic version that it fails adequately to guard against totalitarianism.

A second shared feature of the two theories of law and state earlier identified concerned the source of political authority. In the Thomistic system the synthesis of the Greek and Christian ground-motives necessitates that nature be perfected by divine grace. The state is part of the natural realm and, therefore, requires grace in the form of the church to perfect its nature.[89] The call to do justice addressed to authorities in the public sphere is, as we have seen, grounded in the God-given diversity of the normative aspects of creation, in this case the juridical or 'justitial' aspect. Accordingly, the state derives its God-given authority directly for its inner normative nature; it does not require a super-added grace for its perfection. According to Kuyper, the state was a 'post-fall ordinance', instituted as a response to the disintegrating effects of the fall on the organic unity of society.' Although initially accepting his view, Dooyeweerd, according to Clouser, changed his mind and agreed with Aquinas that the task of a community charged with promoting the common good or public justice is an original creation mandate. Only the necessity of military power to enforce its mandate is an effect of the Fall.[90]

In respect of the third point of similarity, the Thomistic concept of the common good is considered by PCI to be too vague to provide a delimiting criterion of the state and its activity. The reason given for its vagueness is that the concept is also applied to 'lower' human communities as well as to the state and therefore does not serve as an adequate criterion for differentiating the state from other communities.[91] As will be explained below, PCI employs the modal theory of the aspects to identify the juridical normative aspect as the qualifying function of the state community. It is the role played by this aspect, expressed in the concept of public justice, that differentiates it from all other communities.

Notwithstanding some important similarities, there appears to be a fundamental difference between the two 'Christian' conceptions of society. PCI rejects the Thomist natural law conception as expressing an insufficiently biblical view of human society. It also rejects the Thomist dualistic conception of the human person with which its conception of society is connected. In the reformational philosophy there is no natural rational law corresponding to a natural rational component of the human person. The rational is but one amongst a diversity of normative aspects of human existence, all of which find their deeper point of convergence in the human heart. All dimensions of human existence, including the rational, are therefore radically affected by the religious direction(s) which motivate human creatures; out of the heart are the issues of life (Proverbs 4:23).

This section has outlined a critique of the Catholic conceptions of the common good, subsidiarity, and the view of society and the human person on which those conceptions are based. This critique can now be related specifically to the *Statement*'s treatment of law, justice and the state.

Law, Justice and the State in the Churches' *Statement*

The Common Good, Subsidiarity and Supplementation

The common good, and the accompanying principles of subsidiarity and supplementation are employed in the *Statement* to define the role of the state and its laws in promoting the biblical idea of social justice. The entire section dealing with the task of government (§§.26-33) is headed 'The Common Good'. It commences with the following:

> A just society is one in which its members and its structures serve the common good. In this, government plays a vital role. (§.26)

The *Statement* then proceeds to define the role of government as primarily one of serving the common good. It rejects the market-liberal conception of the state or 'government' as being confined to the minimal functions of national security and law and order. Government's 'wider purpose' of serving the common good is:

> ... to secure and protect the dignity of every citizen. Therefore government is to provide conditions where each is enabled to respect the rights of others, and where each can enjoy freedom and fulfilment in the economic, political and cultural life of the nation. (§.26)

This definition of the role of government and its leading idea of the common good is expanded using the terminology of contemporary 'rights-talk'. Further explication of the common good, however, identifies the *Statement*'s conception of government as a distinctly Catholic one.[92] The *Statement* refers to the universal aspect of the principle of the common good –

> [T]he task of working for the common good is not for government only. Economic and political policies are everybody's concern. All are called to become informed, active and responsible participants in economic and political processes. (§.30)

– but also recognises the need to define the distinctive manner in which the state contributes to the common good through the principles of subsidiarity and supplementation.

> Two complementary principles guide government in securing the common good and the wellbeing of citizens. (§.27)

The first principle, subsidiarity:

> ... requires that government undertake only those activities which exceed the capacity of individuals or private groups acting independently .... [I]t calls for a combination of de-centralisation, community initiative and mutual co-operation.

The second principle, supplementation:

> ... requires that government assist communities and individuals to contribute more effectively to social wellbeing, and supplement their activity when the demands of justice exceed their capacities. (§.27)

This conception of the common good with its accompanying principles is supposed to avoid the two extremes of totalitarianism and 'the free market' approach which places human wellbeing at the mercy of economic forces alone' (§.29). Furthermore, the task of promoting the common good is not confined to government. It requires every person to participate responsibly in economic and political processes (§.30). The payment of taxes is an important way in which all contribute to the common good. Governments may rightfully levy such taxes and citizens have a moral duty to pay them. By such a system of fair taxation significant disparities between rich and poor can be avoided (§§.32-33).

The goal of attaining justice in society through the justice-promoting activity of both the state and its citizens is an aspiration shared by many people, Christian or otherwise. The critical question, however, is whether this Thomist conception of government and society, which the *Statement* proposes as the means for attaining that goal, is adequate. Having already examined this conception of society in the earlier discussion of Thomistic theory, we can now apply the results of that examination to a critique of the *Statement*.

One of the major criticisms of the Thomistic view of society mentioned earlier stated that its conception of the common good was too vague or ill-defined to provide an adequate criterion for defining the inner nature of different kinds of human communities. This was because of the manner in which the common good was applied to 'lower' social groupings as well as to the state. The *Statement* applies the concept of the common good in exactly the same manner. As we have seen, according to the *Statement*, not only the state, but everyone (groups as well as individuals) has a responsibility to promote the common good.

The criticism regarding the Thomistic interpretation of the principle of subsidiarity also applies to the *Statement*. The suggested response, following Chaplin, however, was not to abandon the idea of subsidiarity itself but to give it a non-hierarchical or 'horizontal' interpretation according to which each community, including the state, is recognised as possessing its own distinctive character. This involves a qualitative, rather than a quantitative, differentiation.[93]

Similarly, the *Statement* views the principle of subsidiarity as anti-centralist and anti-totalitarian in its implications (as well as countering free-market, minimalist notions of the state) (§§.28 and 29). The principle implies decentralisation, community initiative and mutual co-operation (§.27). Whilst the principle of subsidiarity in the *Statement* implies a limitation on the capacity of non-state societal structures and communities, it implies no similar limitation on the state's *capacity* to act. Does the principle of supplementation remedy this problem?

The principle of supplementation was not considered in the earlier discussion of the Thomistic conception of society and the state. However, it is susceptible to the same criticism that applies to the principle of subsidiarity. It is, after all, a corollary of the latter principle. Subsidiarity defines the limit of the state's capacity to intervene in other communities and in individual lives. The principle of supplementation positively defines the kind of activity the state may undertake to help supplement the activities of those other groups and individuals so they may attain the goal of contributing to the common good.[94]

From the standpoint of PCI, the same difficulty is encountered with this principle as with the principle of subsidiarity. The principle of supplementation is supposed to limit the *purposes* for which that capacity is utilised. But the conception of society on which the principle depends fails to provide an adequate delimitation of the inner nature of the different social spheres. Only by such a delimitation is it possible to posit a principle which can limit the *manner* in which the state acts, as well as the purposes, however broad (e.g. social justice, social harmony) or narrow (promotion of public health, education, welfare, housing, etc.). In this view, only by having regard to the distinctive character of the different normative social spheres will the twin dangers of totalitarianism and the inequities resulting from free-market liberalism be avoided. The principle of sphere sovereignty, as earlier explained, reflects this insight into the nature of the different social spheres. When combined with the insights into the interdependent nature of societal communities contained in the Catholic principle of subsidiarity, the principle of sphere sovereignty offers a rich account of the complex structures of society, their interrelationships and normative character.

Social Justice

The criticism of vagueness that was levelled against the conception of common good may also be levelled against the *Statement*'s notion of 'social justice' itself.[95] This criticism is not merely a logical consequence of the above criticisms of 'the common good' and its accompanying principles.

Use of the phrase 'social justice' tends to imply that justice is a general concept encompassing different kinds of justice of which social justice is one kind. The question then may be asked as to what kind of justice does the qualification 'social' allude? The *Statement* answers this question by defining social justice as:

> (a) fairness in our dealings with other people;
> (b) fairness in the way responsibilities are shared;
> (c) fairness in the distribution of income, wealth and power in our society;
> (d) fairness in the social, economic and political structures we have created;
> (e) fairness in the operation of those structures so that they enable all citizens to be active and productive participants in the life of society. (§.3)

Leaving aside the problem of defining 'fairness', such is the comprehensiveness of this definition that it leaves little scope for a category of justice that does not fall into the broad category of social justice. The definition encompasses not only political structures and other social institutions but all persons in their interpersonal dealings. If social justice, then, is simply meant to refer to the biblical call to justice in all personal and social relations, it is not apparent what purpose is served by adding the qualification 'social'. It might be argued that the qualification is justified in order to distinguish the requirement of justice in human terms from some notion of divine justice. If this is the case then the word 'social' is not an appropriate way of making the distinction.

One justification that has been offered for abandoning talk of justice in favour of social justice is that 'justice' evokes a negative reaction from many who have been the recipients of legal justice administered under the prevailing legal system.[96] Surely, however, the social fact of deficiencies in the administration of legal justice is an insufficient reason for abandoning either use of the term, 'justice' or the concept itself, in its unqualified form, when considering its political and social dimensions? The deficiencies of a legal system are, rather, a reason for calling upon the legal system and its laws to approximate more closely the normative requirements of justice however they may be defined. It makes little sense to reserve the term justice for that which the legal system actually delivers to its members and social justice for what ought to obtain in society, including its legal system.

This criticism might be considered nitpicking. However, the problem of defining social justice is similar to, and connected with, the problem of the common good. The latter problem, as has been argued from the standpoint of PCI, presents a serious deficiency in the *Statement*'s attempt to define the responsibility of the state with regard to the calling of justice.

The common good in Catholic social teaching is supposed to define the functions of the state. Because it is also applied to other social groupings it was argued above that the concept insufficiently characterises the inner nature of the state. The same may be said of the concept of social justice. The concept appears to be primarily directed at the responsibilities of government, yet it is applied to all persons and groupings in society as well. Applying our earlier critique, it can be argued that the deficiencies of both the 'common good' and of 'social justice' arise out of a view of society and its communities which fails to define adequately the inner nature of the different spheres of society and human relationships found within them. The result is a failure to differentiate sufficiently the nature of different societal institutions and organisations in a way that enables the formulation of principles and policies defining the tasks appropriate to each.

The Role of Law, Justice and the State: an Alternative View

According to PCI, because the state is the only human institution which has the justitial as its qualifying or leading function, the kind of justice which the state is called upon to deliver is of a typically 'public-legal' character. The principle or norm of public justice, defining the inner nature of the state, sets a normative limit to the capacities and activities of the state with regard to other societal institutions, communities and relationships. Implementation of this principle would prevent the state from seeking to violate the internal spheres of those non-state communities in recognition of the principle of sphere sovereignty. But this does not mean that the state is prohibited from 'intervening' in any non-state sphere, for example where those communities are failing to realise their own normative callings characterised by their leading or qualifying functions. The state may, for example, have to act in the place of human parents (in *loco parentis*) where they fail to meet the *minimum* ethical requirements of parental love and nurture. The justitial normative qualification of the state's structure means that it can only do so in the interests of justice and in a legal manner. The same holds true for other societal communities. In promoting the public interest the state may, by statutory regulation, make provision for state schools or state business enterprises. But in neither of these two examples will the institutions function in a healthy fashion unless they are free to pursue their respective goals according to the norms and principles appropriate for each type of institution. In this approach it is the distinctive nature of the state's legal dimension or functioning which differentiates it from all other societal structures and which defines and limits its capacities.[97]

One of the major tasks of the state is to integrate the internal legal spheres (law) of non-state communities and institutions, and the juridical interactions of individuals and communities, in a public legal manner.[98] This requires a regime of common legal rules which bind the private law spheres to principles of equity, certainty and fairness, to principles of private law justice. In a 'common law'[99] system such as exists in New Zealand, 'private' law includes the law of contract and tort (civil wrong), and the principles and rules of equity and restitution applicable to private transactions. In the legal theory of PCI a distinction is made between the private law internal to each of the different non-state social spheres and the so-called 'private' law of the state.

The latter is only private in the sense that it has the specific function of integrating the internal law found in non-state social spheres. For example, the law of contract binds private economic transactions (contracts) to a public legal regime to ensure that the parties, when entering into such agreements or when enforcing them, observe common principles of contractual justice. This entails upholding principles of sanctity of contract and freedom of contract as well as moral-legal principles prohibiting unconscionable behaviour in the making of the contract. Where a court adjudges that one of the parties has broken one or more terms of the contract, principles of private justice ensure that the remedies awarded are equitable.[100] What differentiates the private law of the state from the private law found *within* non-state spheres is that it is a *common* law integrating all those non-state legal spheres in a public fashion through laws created and administered by the state's organs – the courts and legislature.

One of the major criticisms which PCI legal theory levels against legal positivism is that its preoccupation with *state* law, as the paradigm of all law, has resulted in overlooking this fundamental distinction between the common law of the state created in carrying out its public legal function of integrating the private legal regimes of non-state spheres, and those private legal regimes themselves. A consequence of legal positivism's influence in legal theory and practice has been a tendency to devalue systems of law other than the state's. This is illustrated in the New Zealand context by the general lack of interest, until recently, in the customary law of the Maori.[101]

Employing his theory of the modal aspects, Dooyweerd explained the private law internal to non-state spheres as an expression of the juridical or justitial modal aspect functioning within that sphere. A contract is the result of a law-making act internal to the sphere of freely interacting persons (inter-individual, or inter-communal – for example, between two companies) in economic relations. The principle of sphere sovereignty and the irreducible nature of the modal aspects ensures there is a normative limit to the state's law interference with the internal law-making function of the sphere concerned. The 'private' common law of the state merely ensures that in exercising that private law-making capacity the parties to a contract, for example, observe common principles of equity, fairness, good faith, etc. The state is authorised to do this because its authority is grounded in the normative qualifying aspect (justitial), which characterises its internal structure and the task which it has to perform.

Public law is the law of the state concerned with the internal organisation of the state itself and the regulation of the relationship between its citizens and those exercising state authority (constitutional law), review of the process of its administrative structures (administrative law) guided by principles of 'natural justice', and all matters aimed at promoting the public interest[102] (e.g. social welfare, health, education, etc.). In PCI's theory of law and state, public legal justice embodies a principle of distributive justice.[103] The latter requires, amongst other things, that there are no excessive disparities of wealth and income which result in poverty or oppressive conditions for some individuals and communities. It may require the state to impose an obligation on the wealthier to contribute to the needs of the poor and disadvantaged by means of taxation. The biblical testimony to the principle of distributive justice and the responsibility of public authorities for its application are well known.[104]

Family law and law of marriage and unmarried cohabitation is an example of an area of law which aims at promoting the public interest. It does this by giving support to what the state regards as the normative (healthy) functioning of these institutions and by regulating the legal relationships of the parties in the event of a breakdown of the family or marital relationships, according to principles of marital and family justice. Concrete applications of these principles are contained in the laws relating to the division of property and the maintenance and custody of children.

In summary, justice is a creational requirement sourced in God's normative ordering. This norm applies to all persons in their communal, intercommunal and interpersonal relationships and to all communities in their dealings with their own members and with other communities. Its social function is expressed in the duties and rules formed within all of these relationships. Even a family has its own rules of behaviour for ensuring fairness. But, it is only the state which is characterised by its calling to do justice and to address injustice by means of regimes of public and private (common) law.

The above outline of an alternative theory of law and state and justice is offered as providing possible solutions for problems identified in the *Statement*'s treatment of these topics. In this theory, human communities of whatever type contribute to the 'common good' and to the attainment of justice in society by observing the principle of sphere sovereignty or sphere integrity. This principle does not inhibit interrelations and interconnections amongst the various social groupings and institutions. Rather, it is intended to limit the manner of those interactions in a way that preserves the integrity of each grouping and institution according to its own inner nature.

Conclusion

The *Statement*'s conception of the common good and the accompanying principles of subsidiarity and supplementation are based on an hierarchical view of society which fails to provide an adequate account of the inner normative nature of different social spheres. The state is only one type of social structure, not the highest expression of human society in the natural sphere. Nevertheless, the state's contribution to the attainment of justice in society is a critical one. Only that institution has the task of providing a regime of public justice as part of its inner nature. All other communities contribute to social justice to the extent that they realise the justitial-legal aspect of their inner nature. But only the state has the role of integrating all these legal spheres by means of its system of laws. The approach adopted in this chapter has rejected some of the assumptions implicit in the *Statement*'s adoption of the principles of common good, subsidiarity and supplementation. Yet, it has also recognised that the principles themselves, and the Catholic teaching upon which they are based, have made an important contribution toward the articulation of a theory of social justice based on biblical principles.

Notes

1. For historical background see Bernard Zylstra's Introduction to L. Kalsbeek, *Contours of a Christian Philosophy,* Toronto: Wedge, 1975.
2. See D. Caudill, *Disclosing Tilt,* Amsterdam: Free University Press, 1989, p. 83.
3. For a recent defence and development of this idea of religion see R.A. Clouser, *The Myth of Religious Neutrality,* Indiana: University of Notre Dame Press, 1991.
4. See D.L. Roper, *Biblical Foundations for Radical Discipleship,* Wellington, 1977, for an exposition of this theme.
5. For example, H. Ridderbos, *The Coming of the Kingdom,* Philadelphia: Presbyterian and Reformed, 1975.
6. Dooyeweerd's major work is *De Wijsbegeerte der Wetsidee* (1935-1936), the English translation of which is contained in *A New Critique of Theoretical Thought,* Philadelphia: Presbyterian and Reformed, 4 vol. 1953-58.
7. This is the so-called 'transcendental' critique. Ibid., vol. 1, pp. 3-21, 34ff.
8. Ibid., p. 57.
9. Ibid., p. 20.
10. Clouser, *The Myth of Religious Neutrality*, pp. 21-24.
11. As opposed to 'transcendent', a transcendental critique is one which, having identified the fundamental religious basis and philosophical assumptions of the theory or theoretical tradition, examines the inner structure of that thought in the light of those religious and philosophical assumptions. A transcendent critique, on the other hand, is one which simply criticises from a position outside of the theory or tradition examined without giving a critical account of the internal (immanent) structure of the position examined and its deepest presuppositions based on religious beliefs. See Dooyeweerd, *A New Critique of Theoretical Thought,* vol. 1, pp. 37-38.
12. Ibid., pp. 61-66.

13. Ibid., p. 61.
14. H. Dooyeweerd, *A New Critique of Theoretical Thought,* Philadelphia: Presbyterian and Reformed, 4 vol. 1953-58.
15. For an account of the scholastic ground-motive and its dialectical character see ibid., p. 172ff.
16. For Dooyeweerd's discussion of the relationship between religious ground-motives and ground-ideas see ibid., p. 68ff and pp. 190-92.
17. This is a summary of Dooyeweerd's detailed analysis in Part II, Vol. I of 'The Development of the Basic Antinomy' in the ground-idea or 'Cosmonomic Idea of Humanistic Immanence Philosophy', ibid., vol. 1, p.169ff.
18. See E. Schuurman, *Reflections on the Technological Society,* Toronto: Wedge, 1977, p. 53ff.
19. H. Dooyeweerd, *Roots of Western Culture*, Toronto: Wedge, 1979, pp. 153-55, 171, 173, 194; *idem, A New Critique of Theoretical Thought*, vol. 1, p. 216ff.; vol. 2, p. 360; vol. 3, p. 232.
20. Ibid., vol. 1, pp. 57-64.
21. Ibid., p. 61.
22. For an explanation of the idea of immanence philosophy see ibid., p. 12ff.
23. Ibid., p. 35. See also *idem, The Twilight of Western Thought,* Nutley, N.J.: Craig Press, 1972.
24. Dooyeweerd, *A New Critique of Theoretical Thought*, vol. 1, pp. 37-38.
25. For an extensive treatment of these problems see H. Dooyeweerd, *In the Twilight of Western Thought*, Nutley, N.J.: Craig Press, 1972, pp. 113-172.
26. For a detailed treatment of the nature of revelation and its implications for a Christian world-view see B.J. van der Walt, *The Liberating Message: A Christian Worldview for Africa*, Potchefstroom: Institute for Reformational Studies, Potchefstroom University for Christian Higher Education, 1994, pp. 56-89.
27. Ibid., p. 71ff.
28. Dooyeweerd, *A New Critique of Theoretical Thought,* vol. 1, p. 68ff for the role of ground-ideas.
29. Ibid., p. 69.
30. For a summary of this point and the three problems see Dooyeweerd in his 'first way' to a critique of theoretical thought. Ibid., pp. 3-21.
31. Dooyeweerd and his followers have preferred the term 'Cosmonomic Idea' in translating the original Dutch term 'wetsidee' which literally means 'law-idea' in order to avoid confusion with the specifically juridical sense of the term. See Kalsbeek, *Contours of a Christian Philosophy*, p. 69.
32. For a discussion of the idea of God's Word as law and the debate over its nature and role in PCI see van der Walt, *The Liberating Message*, pp. 130-42.
33. For a detailed analysis of the ground-idea of humanistic immanence philosophy, ibid., vol. 1, p. 169ff. And for a summary comparison of the Christian ground-idea and the humanistic, ibid., pp. 501-08.
34. For the questions and answers see Dooyeweerd, *A New Critique of Theoretical Thought*, vol. 1, 99ff.
35. Ibid.

36. The very first sentence of *A New Critique* refers to the modal aspects. Ibid., p. 3.
37. For example, the exact number and order of the aspects and Dooyeweerd's categorisation of aspects into normative and non-normative. See M.D. Stafleu, 'Criteria for a Law Sphere (with special emphasis on the 'psychic' modal sphere)', *Philosophia Reformata*, 53/2, 1988, pp. 170-85.
38. Kalsbeek, *Contours of a Christian Philosophy*, pp. 20-21.
39. Encyclopaedie van de Rechtswetenschap (3 vol.) unpublished, 1961-1967.
40. Dooyeweerd insisted on maintaining a distinction between the branches of philosophy (philosophy of law, philosophy of ethics, etc.) which investigated the philosophical problems underlying the various special disciplines or sciences (law, ethics, etc.) and the special theoretical concepts unique to each discipline which proceed on the basis of answers to those philosophical problems. Hence, it was important to make a distinction between philosophy of law (philosophical problems underlying the special concepts of law) and jurisprudence (legal concepts), The Anglo-American tradition of law generally does not insist on this sharp distinction, often including philosophy of law in the term jurisprudence and vice versa.
41. A significant part of his contribution in these areas have been made available in English through the publications of Dooyeweerd's successor to the Chair in Jurisprudence, the late Prof. H.J. van Eikema Hommes who devoted his efforts to disseminating and applying Dooyeweerd's theoretical work in philosophy of law and jurisprudence. See H.J. Hommes, *Major Trends in the History of Legal Philosophy*, Amsterdam: North Holland, 1979. Much of Dooyeweerd's jurisprudential works are still in the process of being translated from the original Dutch.
42. Dooyeweerd, *A New Critique*, ibid., vol. 3, pp. 379-506; *idem, The Christian Idea of the State,* Nutley, N.J.: Craig Press, 1968.
43. For an introduction to the theory of the modal aspects and the role of theory see Kalsbeek, *Contours of a Christian Philosophy,* pp. 35-66, 84ff.
44. Dooyeweerd, *A New Critique of Theoretical Thought*, vol. 2, p. 237ff.
45. See Kalsbeek, *Contours of a Christian Philosophy*, pp. 119-25 on the subject-object relation. For a helpful explanation of this aspect of the theory in terms of active and passive functions see Clouser, *The Myth of Religious Neutrality*, p. 212ff.
46. A thing can function in a modal aspect as an object. For example, a stone functions as a biotic object for a living creature such as a bird or an animal which uses stones as an implement. For other examples see Kalsbeek, *Contours of a Christian Philosophy*, p. 122ff.
47. For an introduction to the theory of the structures of human society, ibid., pp. 196-268.
48. For Dooyeweerd's theory of human structures see *A New Critique of Theoretical Thought*, vol. 3, pp. 157ff. and Kalsbeek, *Contours of a Christian Philosophy*, pp. 196ff.
49. Stafleu differs from Dooyeweerd by including non-human creatures, such as animals, along with human persons as creatures having *subject* functions in the higher aspects. He argues that animals are capable of loving and, therefore, function subjectively in the ethical aspect. But only humans function normatively in these higher aspects; that is, only men and women have responsibility for abiding by norms of love, justice, faithfulness, economy, etc. On this view, 'normative' is not a correct description of the higher aspects. Stafleu, 'Criteria for a Law Sphere', *Philosophia Reformata*, p. 177.

50. In PCI it is important to distinguish this temporal moral aspect of human experience from the central religious commandment of divine love. Dooyeweerd, *A New Critique of Theoretical Thought,* vol. 2, p. 144ff.
51. H. Dooyeweerd, *The Roots of Western Culture*, p. 125.
52. Kalsbeek, *Contours of a Christian Philosophy*, p. 206.
53. For an excellent recent account of the PCI conception of norms and normativity see van der Walt, *The Liberating Message,* pp. 134-140.
54. Neil MacCormick, 'Law as Institutional Fact' in N. MacCormick and O. Weinberger (eds), *An Institutional Theory of Law,* Dordrecht: D. Reidel Publishing, 1986.
55. 'Juridical' is Dooyeweerd's term (followed by Hommes), Clouser prefers 'justitial' to reflect more clearly the normative meaning of justice or fairness. Clouser, *The Myth of Religious Neutrality,* pp. 205, 207.
56. Ibid., pp. 270ff.
57. See P.A. Joseph, *Constitutional and Administrative Law in New Zealand*, Sydney: The Law Book Company, 1993, pp. 167ff, who describes the doctrine as 'the sentinel of constitutional government', p. 167.
58. This is the theory of sphere universality for a summary of which see Kalsbeek, ibid., pp. 109-13.
59. Ibid., pp. 102 and *A New Critique of Theoretical Thought*, ibid., vol. 2, p. 129 ff.
60. In a discussion during the 14th World Conference of the International Association for Philosophy of Law and Social Philosophy (IVR) in 1989.
61. Clouser, *The Myth of Religious Neutrality*, pp. 205, 207.
62. In the nineteenth century and the early part of the this century, that dominance has been attributed to Jeremy Bentham, John Austin and their followers. From about the middle of this century its influence is largely owing to the seminal work of H.L.A. Hart, *The Concept of Law*, Oxford: Oxford University Press, 1961. For one of the many accounts of modern legal positivism and its predecessors see R. Cotterell, *The Politics of Jurisprudence: A Critical Introduction to Legal Philosophy,* London: Butterworths, 1989, pp. 52-117.
63. Hart, *The Concept of Law*, pp. 92-120.
64. R. Dworkin, *Taking Rights Seriously*, London: Duckworth, 1977; *Law's Empire,* London: Fontana, 1986.
65. CLS is more a movement than a school. It draws on a diverse range of intellectual sources. In the original North American version an important antecedent is Amercian legal realism. Other important sources are sociology of knowledge, German Critical Theory and radical literary theory. See Caudill, *Disclosing Tilt*, pp. 37-53.
66. For a perceptive account of postmodern legal theory by a CLSer of the neo-Marxist type see Alan Hunt, 'The Big Fear: Law Confronts Postmodernism', *McGill Law Journal*, 35/3, 1990, pp. 509-40.
67. An example of a CLS critique of Dworkin is J.M. Balkin, 'Taking Ideology Seriously: Ronald Dworkin and the CLS critique', 55/3 *UMKC Law Review,* 1987, pp. 392-433.
68. M. Urlich, 'A Short Topology of Feminist Legal Theory' *Auckland University Law Review*, 7/2 1993, pp. 483-89.
69. See Caudill, *Disclosing Tilt*, 81-121 for a comparison of the Critical Legal Studies' ideology critique with that of PCI.
70. See Hommes, *Major Trends,* p. 371ff. He describes the method of analysis contained in the legal theory of PCI as 'transcendental-empirical', ibid., pp. 372-74.

71. On principles see H.J. van Eikema Hommes, 'Positive Law and Material-Legal Principles', *Archiv fur Rechts-und Sozialphilosophie* 70/2, 1984 pp. 153-70; on human rights see P. Marshall, *Human Rights Theories in Christian Perspective*, Toronto: Institute for Christian Studies, 1983 and on private legal rights, J. van der Vyver, 'The Doctrine of Private-Law Rights' in Strauss (ed.), *Huldingingsbundel vir WA Joubert*, 1988, pp. 201-46.
72. For a critique of legal positivism see the analysis of Hart's 'rule of recognition' in Hommes, *Major Trends in Legal Philosophy*, pp. 363-64.
73. Ibid., pp. 50-1.
74. See Dooyeweerd, *The Roots of Western Culture*, pp. 25-6 (Roman and Greek), pp. 115-132 (Roman Catholic), pp. 148ff (humanistic); Hommes, *Major Trends in the History of Legal Philosophy*, pp. 3-156.
75. Dooyeweerd, *The Roots of Western Culture*, p. 122.
76. Ibid., p.123.
77. Ibid., p.124.
78. For a detailed comparison of the differences and similarities between the Catholic conception of state and society found in the papal encyclicals, beginning with *Rerum Novarum* (1891) and the Dutch reformational conception contained in PCI see Jonathan Chaplin, 'Subsidiarity and Sphere Sovereignty: Catholic and Reformed Conceptions of the Role of the State' in F.P. McHugh and S.M. Natale (eds), *Things Old and New: Catholic Social Teaching Revisited*, Lanham: University Press of America, 1993, pp. 175-202.
79. For a concise account of the principle in the European context and some of its implications see Karlheinz Neunreither, 'Subsidiarity as a Guiding Principle for European Community Activities' in *Government and Opposition* 28/2, 1993, pp. 206-220, esp. pp. 206-7.
80. *The Roots of Western Culture*, p. 125. For other accounts see Chaplin, 'Subsidiarity and Sphere Sovereignty', p. 178ff. and Chapter 5 below.
81. Chaplin, 'Subsidiarity and Sphere Sovereignty', p. 188.
82. Dooyeweerd, *The Roots of Western Culture*, p. 125.
83. The Dutch phrase he used was 'souvereiniteit in eigen kring', literally translated as 'sovereignty in one's own sphere'. Renowned for his criticism of the French Revolution and its motivating spirit, van Prinsterer became leader of the 'Anti-revolutionary' party in the Dutch Parliament. An English translation of his critique is found in *Unbelief and Revolution* 2 vol., Amsterdam: The Groen van Prinsterer Fund, 1973, 1975.
84. For an account of Kuyper's formulation of the principle see Chaplin, 'Subsidiarity and Sphere Sovereignty', pp. 188-91. For a comparison of the ideas of subsidiarity and common good with the idea of sphere sovereignty see ibid., 178ff.
85. Ibid., pp. 124-26.
86. Ibid., p. 129.
87. Chaplin, 'Subsidiarity and Sphere Sovereignty', p. 192.
88. Ibid., pp. 186-7, 192-93.
89. Dooyeweerd, *The Roots of Western Culture*, p. 129.

90. Clouser, *The Myth of Religious Neutrality*, p. 268, n 5.
91. Dooyweerd, *The Roots of Western Culture*, p. 124.
92. See Chapter 5.
93. Chaplin, 'Subsidiarity and Sphere Sovereignty', p. 193.
94. Chaplin's discussion on the the three kinds of activities (enabling, intervening and substituting) which he takes the principle of subsidiarity to imply for the the role of the state in Catholic social teaching appear to apply equally to the principle of supplementation. Chaplin, 'Subsidiarity and Sphere Sovereignty', pp. 185-86.
95. See also Chapter 3.
96. Bill Atkin made this point in a response to the paper on which this chapter is based. See also Ruth Smithies in Chapter 5, defending the use of 'social justice' in Catholic teaching.
97. Chaplin, 'Subsidiarity and Sphere Sovereignty', p. 194.
98. Dooyeweerd, *A New Critique of Theoretical Thought,* vol. 3, p. 433ff. and Hommes, *Major Trends in Legal Philosophy*, p. 398. In Dooyeweerd's theory of the state, Chaplin finds a distinction between the *internal structure* and the *task* of the state. He maintains that the latter cannot be derived from the former and that Dooyeweerd failed to supply a sufficient criterion for defining the state's *task.* He does not think that Dooyeweerd's conception of public justice as the normative qualification of the state's internal structure is adequate to characterise the distinctive task of that institution. He finds the idea of common good, in the sense of the public interest or general welfare, which Dooyeweerd had criticised in Catholic thought, to be essential for an adequate conception of the state. See Chaplin, 'Subsidiarity and Sphere Sovereignty', pp. 194-96.
99. I.e. by contrast with 'civil law' systems. In legal circles the phrase 'common law' may refer to either the rules and principles first developed by the Royal Courts of Common Law in England or, to the latter *and* the principles and rules called 'equity', first developed and administered by the Court of Chancery.
100. For an excellent account of the manner in which the modern law of contract in New Zealand gives expression to the principle of justice see D.L. McLauchlan, 'The New Law of Contract', *The Recent Law Review,* 1992, pp. 436-61. McLauchlan's account lends support to Dooyeweerd's idea that the private law of civil obligations (i.e. 'common private law') gives effect to principles of justice, that the law seeks to impose 'just solutions which can be ascribed to reasonable people in the position of the parties ...', ibid., p. 439.
101. His Honour, Judge Durie, Chief Judge of the Maori Land Court and Chairperson of the Waitangi Tribunal, has commented on the lack of legal scholarship on the subject. 'Custom Law', Wellington, 20 July 1994, p. 1 (unpublished), address to the Wellington Branch of the New Zealand Society for Legal and Social Philosophy.
102. Chaplin, 'Subsidiarity and Sphere Sovereignty', p. 195, suggests that Dooyeweerd did not adequately develop the idea of the public interest in his theory of the state.
103. Dooyeweerd, *A New Critique of Theoretial Thought*, vol. 3, pp. 444-46.
104. For example, the institutions of sabbath years and Jubilee in Israelite society, Lev 25.

[illegible]

Chapter 3

Love, Justice and the State

Jonathan Boston

> Love can only do more, it can never do less, than justice requires... . The real gift of love only begins where justice has already been done, for it is that which is beyond justice.
>
> Emil Brunner[1]

One of the most important matters touched upon both explicitly and implicitly in the *Social Justice Statement* is the relationship between love and justice. Few issues have been more controversial in the history of Christian social ethics than the question of how love – in the sense of *neighbour love* or *agape*, rather than *philia* (friendship) or *eros* (sexual love) – and justice are related. Are they fundamentally complementary and in harmony, or are they in tension, if not direct opposition to each other? Is it possible to be simultaneously just and merciful? Is retribution consistent with forgiveness? Are social justice and love versions of the same moral norm such that their requirements are identical, or at least compatible? There is no consensus amongst Christian ethicists on such matters.

That love and justice are both crucial ethical imperatives is rarely disputed. God's love for the world, expressed supremely in Christ's life, death and resurrection, is at the very heart of Christian theology.[2] And the two great commandments – that we should love God and love our neighbours as ourselves – set the tone for, and are pivotal to, any distinctively Christian ethics (see Chapter 4).[3] Likewise, a concern for justice, whether understood primarily in terms of fairness or giving people their due (or their rightful place within

God's world), is also central to the Judeo-Christian tradition. God is just, and requires that humanity live justly and actively oppose injustice.

Yet how are love and justice related? Some maintain that love and justice are radically different from, if not alien to, each other in their nature and purpose. Thus, it is impossible in many, if not most, situations to be both loving and just. If this is the case, then one of the immediate questions is which should take precedence: should we be loving *or* just? By contrast, others maintain that love and justice are identical, or at least fundamentally similar in their ultimate purposes. Consequently, love can make the ends of justice its own and justice can serve the ends of love.

A related, and equally controversial issue, is whether love is relevant to the public or social realm (such as the actions of groups, organisations and states), or whether it is by definition confined to the private or personal sphere. In other words, can love be expressed through institutional forms and arrangements such as laws, political organisations, and public bureaucracies? Similarly, can and should the command to love our neighbours be used to guide the design of public policy? Some Christian ethicists argue that while justice is relevant to both the public and private spheres of life we cannot love indirectly and collectively; we cannot love groups of people most of whom we have never seen; love of neighbour is meaningless except in a direct 'I-Thou' relationship between two persons. Accordingly, it is argued that it is simply inappropriate, if not meaningless, to suggest that groups and nations should act lovingly – for example, that unions should practice forgiveness towards employers, or that nations should act sacrificially in the face of external aggression. Hence, is it erroneous and inconsistent to talk about the loving use of statutory authority, state coercion or military force, perhaps even the loving use of nuclear weapons. Equally, it is wrong to see state activities, such as the provision of education, health care, housing or social assistance (whether universal or means-tested), as instruments or expressions of love. And nor should the payment of taxes be seen as a means whereby people can fulfil the commandment to love their neighbours. After all, it is surely wrong to equate coerced giving with love. From this perspective, then, love is limited to the domain of inter-personal relations; it is justice which is the proper standard for guiding the actions of groups, institutions and nations.

Of course, many Christian ethicists find such reasoning unconvincing. If love cannot be applied to the social and political realm, it implies that crucial Christian ethical principles are irrelevant to much of life. Surely, it is argued, such a position is inconsistent with a moral framework which claims to be universal in its application and with the God revealed to us in Christ who is Lord of all (including governments and nations).

This chapter explores the relationship between love and justice. One of the issues under examination is whether it is justified to conceive of the state as an instrument of love, and whether public policy can and should be guided by the demands of love, mercy and compassion. I will take as my starting point the position advanced by the church leaders in their *Social Justice Statement*. The first part of the chapter sets out the key elements of this *Statement* and endeavours to clarify the authors' approach to the relationship between love and justice. Following this, the chapter examines three different perspectives on love and justice which have had currency within the Christian tradition of social ethics. The three positions are: (a) that love and justice are identical; (b) that love and justice are at times, if not often, in radical opposition; and (c) that love and justice are different, yet compatible and inseparable; love takes a different form or manner in the public and private spheres of life. Most attention is given to the third position, in particular the views of three influential twentieth century Protestant theologians, Emil Brunner,[4] Reinhold Niebuhr,[5] and Helmut Thielicke.[6] Against the backdrop of these views, the chapter examines the merits of the arguments advanced in the *Social Justice Statement*.

The issues under examination here are complex and broad-ranging in nature. They touch on many of the central issues in Christian theology (e.g. the character of God, the nature of the kingdom of God and its social implications, the nature of the ethical teaching of Jesus and the extent to which his ethical ideals can be applied in the present 'fallen' world, and the proper role of the state). In the space of a single chapter it is impossible to provide an exhaustive treatment of all the relevant theological and ethical issues. Necessarily, therefore, this discussion is partial and incomplete. In particular, it ignores the insights and contribution of Catholic social teaching (see Chapter 5), liberation theology and feminist theology. Similarly, it does not attempt to analyse or interpret some of the more controversial biblical material (e.g. the Sermon on the Mount). Nor does it consider in any depth the policy implications arising from the various theological positions under discussion.

The Treatment of Love and Justice in the *Social Justice Statement*

As noted in Chapter 1, the *Social Justice Statement* was essentially a response by the church leadership to the National government's changes in social policy in the early 1990s. Of particular concern were the cuts in welfare benefits, the radical changes to housing assistance, and the imposition of higher user charges in education and health care, and the resultant increase in poverty and human suffering (reflected most visibly in the huge growth in demand for food parcels from voluntary agencies).[7] It is thus a document which arose out of a particular historical context, and seeks to speak prophetically, in the tradition of the Old Testament prophets, into this context.

While the *Statement* endeavours to present a coherent account of the meaning of social justice, it makes no attempt to provide a comprehensive theological analysis of the relationship between love and justice (or love and social justice). Nor does it explore in any detail whether, and how, the commandments to love God and our neighbours should be applied to the social and political realm. Nevertheless, the *Statement* does make some specific comments which pertain to the relationship between love and justice, and the application of neighbour love to the role and policies of the state.[8]

Significantly, the *Statement* commences with the well-known quote from the Old Testament prophet Micah (6.8): 'What does the Lord require of you but to do justice, love kindness and walk humbly with your God?' The *Statement* ignores the broader and unqualified term 'justice'; it likewise avoids any discussion of 'punitive' or 'criminal' justice. Instead, it moves straight to the subject of 'social' justice. This is defined by the church leaders in terms of fairness or distributive justice. That is to say, it is about the fair and proper sharing of responsibilities and benefits. It also entails the pursuit of the common good and the protection of human rights. The *Statement* implies that such rights are based primarily on considerations of human need and the protection of human dignity.

With respect to the relationship between love and justice, the *Statement* makes the following comments:

> We and our Church members seek social justice because we believe that as we serve this goal we truly serve the loving purposes of God. We seek social justice because we worship a just God. We act with compassion because we worship a God who is merciful. (§.4)

> ... Jesus Christ taught the primacy of love. St Paul echoed that teaching when he wrote: 'So faith, hope and love abide, these three; but the greatest of these is love' (I Cor 13.13). The meaning of the word 'love' does not confine it simply to acts of charity. It includes working for justice. Charitable work in the service of those in need

> must go hand in hand with the work to establish just structures so that citizens do not have to depend on acts of charity. (§.14)

> A central emphasis in Christian teaching is the requirement that we love our neighbour with the same self-giving love that Jesus displayed for his disciples. Love binds us together in community. Love is active caring. Through loving and being loved we become mature, fulfilled persons. (§.19)

> Loving as Jesus loves us means that we cannot support pure individualism, where people are encouraged to focus only on their own interests. When economic policies, as at present, encourage selfish individualism a society is created where only the fittest or the fortunate survive, and others become helpless victims of the system. (§.20)

The central arguments made in these and related parts of the *Statement* can be systematised and presented in the following manner:

1. Justice and mercy are rooted in the character of God.
2. For Christians, 'self-giving love' or 'active caring' is of primary importance.
3. Love fosters community and is central to the development of 'mature, fulfilled persons'.
4. To love requires more than individual 'acts of charity'; it also requires 'working for justice'. In other words, love requires justice, but is not limited to the pursuit of justice.
5. Social justice means distributive fairness and the satisfaction of basic human needs.
6. There are at least two reasons why we must pursue social justice: because it serves 'the loving purposes of God' and because God is just. Or to put it differently, God's love for humanity is expressed, at least in part, through just social and political structures. From this perspective, then, the *Statement* suggests that the state is an instrument through which God's love and justice can be expressed (although of course this does not imply that the state is always loving or just). It presumably follows from this that the authors believe that love can, in a sense, be expressed via institutional forms and is directly applicable to the public realm.
7. Christians are obliged to be charitable, but also to 'work to establish just structures so that citizens do not have to depend on acts of charity'. One

obvious implication of this is that if the state's policies were just (or at least more just) there would be much less need for charity (if any need at all). Less clear, however, is the attitude of the church leaders to charitable works. On the one hand the suggestion that public policy should seek to ensure that 'citizens do not have to depend on acts of charity' might be taken to imply that charity is second best and reflects the failings of the state (or collective provision). On the other hand the *Statement* makes it plain that charitable work is a necessary requirement of the great commandments and hence is a virtue. Also, the emphasis given in the *Statement* to the principles of subsidiarity and supplementation (see §§.27, 28 and 44) can leave no doubt that the authors place a high value on voluntary social service and charitable giving, and that they believe that the state must facilitate and encourage voluntary responses to human need.

8. 'Pure individualism', where people pursue only their own interests, is inconsistent with the requirement to love 'as Jesus loves us'. Current economic policies 'encourage selfish individualism', and are therefore wrong. Such statements imply first, that the state can and should discourage selfish individualism, and second, that public policies, including economic policies, should be consistent with the requirements of neighbour love. What precisely this means in practice is not spelled out in the *Statement*. In general terms, however, the authors *may* be suggesting that governments, in designing their public policies, should pose the following question: 'What is the most loving thing to do?' Another way of putting it is to say that the goal of public policy should be to maximise love.
9. Overall, the *Statement* appears to be relatively optimistic about the capacity of governments to achieve social justice, guarantee human rights and minimise poverty. This optimism is highlighted by the suggestion that one of the goals of public policy should be to ensure that 'citizens do not have to depend on acts of charity'. Further, there are few, if any, cautionary remarks about the limitations to state action.

In summary, love and justice are both important; they must go hand in hand. Love requires justice, but is not limited to justice (for it includes charity). Since in pursuing justice one is also fulfilling the requirement to love one's neighbours, just social and political structures can be regarded as an expression of neighbour love. Necessarily, therefore, love has an unquestioned and vital role to play in the public life of a nation; it is not limited to the private or personal sphere of life.

Three Perspectives on the Relationship Between Love and Justice

As noted, moral theologians and other writers on Christian social ethics have advanced a wide range of views on the relationship between love and justice. Three perspectives will be considered here: first, the claim that love and justice are identical; second, the argument that love and justice are, at times, radically opposed and that love must prevail over justice; and third, the view that love and justice, while different, are nonetheless compatible. These three positions, of course, are not exhaustive of those represented within the Christian tradition. Indeed, in the history of Christian social ethics a number of other distinct positions can be identified, as well as variations on the positions noted above.[9]

Position 1: Love and Justice are Identical

According to the first position under consideration, love and justice are more or less identical in nature, there is no tension between them, and both can be applied to the public and private spheres of life. Probably the best known advocate of this position is the American ethicist Joseph Fletcher. In his influential and highly controversial book *Situation Ethics*, Fletcher argues that 'Love and justice are the same, for justice is love distributed; nothing else'.[10] Hence, love and justice are not to be seen as opposites, alternatives or complements; rather they are identical. As he variously puts it:

> ... love does more than take justice into account, it *becomes* justice ...[11] Justice is the many-sidedness of love ... Love is justice, justice is love ...[12] They are one and the same. To be loving is to be just. To be just is to be loving ...[13] Justice is nothing other than love working out its problems ... [or] coping with situations where distribution is called for ... Justice is Christian love using its head, calculating its duties, obligations, opportunities, resources.[14]

How does Fletcher reach such surprising, if not counter-intuitive, conclusions? Part of the explanation lies in his understanding of love. Rather than seeing love as being unconditional, extravagant, uncalculating, or even non-rational, Fletcher maintains that love is 'careful', 'diligent' and 'prudent'.[15] As he expresses it, 'Prudence and love are not just partners, they are one and the same ... since they both go out to others'.[16] Further, he argues that:

> ... love's outreach is many-sided and wide-aimed, not one-directional; it is pluralist, not monist; multilateral, not unilateral. Agapeic love is not a one-to-one affair. (That would be *philia* or *eros.*) ... Faced as we always are in the social complex with a web of duties ... love is compelled to be calculating, careful, prudent, distributive.[17]

Once love is seen in this way, it is a somewhat shorter logical step than would otherwise be the case to regarding it as justice.

The second reason for the conclusion that love and justice are identical, lies in his understanding of justice. Suppose, Fletcher argues, that we accept that justice is giving to everyone their due (or their rights). What is their due? According to Fletcher, the Christian answer is simple: 'It is love that is due – *only* love'.[18] If doing justice to our neighbours means to love them, it follows that love and justice are one and the same thing.

From Fletcher's perspective, therefore, love and justice are not at variance and cannot be separated. Nor is it proper to think of love as requiring more than justice or going beyond the demands of justice. On the contrary, to do more than justice requires would be simultaneously unjust and unloving. Neither is love particular and justice general, but each one is both. Given this approach, Fletcher rejects any suggestion that love might be limited to the personal or private sphere (such as the care of an *immediate* neighbour) and justice to the social or public sphere. As he puts it, 'To say that love is between individuals and justice between groups, and that a union cannot 'love' a corporation or a city cannot love the nation, is to sentimentalise love and dehumanise justice'.[19] On the contrary, love applies equally to relationships between individuals as it does to 'union-management relations, international affairs, trade treaties, United Nations policy and the like'.[20]

But how can organisations, institutions and states act lovingly? What implications does the imperative to love have for the role of the state and the design of public policy? Fletcher's answer is that the love ethic must 'form a coalition with utilitarianism'.[21] Rather than seeking the 'greatest good for the greatest number', as Jeremy Bentham and John Stuart Mill maintained, governments should seek the 'greatest amount of neighbour welfare for the largest number of neighbours possible'.[22] How this principle should be applied in practice (e.g. with respect to the amount of income redistribution, or the design of a country's education, health and criminal justice systems) is not addressed in any detail by Fletcher. What is plain, however, is that Fletcher considers that it is perfectly consistent with the requirements of love for a state to engage in enforced redistribution or to use lethal force to achieve its ends.

Some of Fletcher's views on love and justice have found a degree of support amongst other Christian ethicists. Macquarrie, for instance, concurs with Fletcher's view that 'It is a false disjunction that suggests an opposition between justice and love'.[23] Likewise, Forrester and Skene, although rejecting the proposition that love and justice are exactly the same, endorse Fletcher's contention that justice can be viewed as 'love distributed, the way in which a community loves its members'.[24] Or again: 'Doing justice and loving are, in both Old and New Testaments, complementary descriptions of the same kind of behaviour'.[25]

An advocate of position 1, like Fletcher, would find some aspects of the *Social Justice Statement* thoroughly acceptable. In particular, the *Statement* is consistent with position 1 in supporting the contention that love requires the pursuit of justice and that love can be applied in the public sphere; it is not limited to private acts of charity. Further, to the extent that the *Statement* implies that policy-makers should always seek to do the most loving thing, it would be in accord with Fletcher's view. The *Statement* and position 1 would also seem to be similarly optimistic with respect to the capacity of governments to secure justice and the capacity of individuals and groups to fulfil the requirements of neighbour love. Against this, the *Statement* is fundamentally at odds with position 1 in the distinction which it draws between the meaning of love and justice and its implicit rejection of the view that love and justice are identical. Plainly, unlike Fletcher, the authors of the *Statement* believe that love is a different and arguably more demanding ethical standard than justice.

A Brief Critique

Despite the simplicity and superficial attractiveness of Fletcher's position, his arguments are open to numerous criticisms.[26] There is space to consider only a few of them here.

First and foremost, Fletcher's definitions of love and justice are highly questionable. The suggestion that *agape* should be viewed as 'careful', 'diligent' and 'prudent'[27] rather than self-giving, sacrificial, unconditional, uncalculating, or spontaneous accords neither with the general weight of scholarly opinion nor with common usage.[28] Neighbour love is not disinterested, remote, cool, generalised benevolence, but committed, generous, compassionate, and at times affectionate care for another person. It delights in another's good, and endures without limit (see 1 Cor 13). This is highlighted by the examples of neighbour love commended by Jesus. In the parable of the prodigal son (Luke

15: 11-32) the father takes no account of the son's wayward behaviour and spontaneously and unbegrudgingly welcomes him home. There is no suggestion that the father's joy, forgiveness and generosity is born of a prudent, calculating or careful mind. In a like fashion, the good Samaritan (Luke 10: 30-36) responds immediately to the need of the man who has been beaten and robbed on the road from Jerusalem to Jericho; he takes little heed of his own wellbeing or the risks he faces in stopping to help his neighbour. Similarly, against the calculating, prudent opposition of his disciples, Jesus commends the woman who movingly and extravagantly anoints him in Bethany (Mark 14: 3-9; Matt. 26: 6-13; John 12: 1-8). It is perhaps unsurprising that Fletcher regards the disciples' attitude, rather than that of Jesus and the woman, as the more loving.[29]

Equally problematic are Fletcher's claims that justice is no more than love distributed and that giving people their due means simply and solely to love them. For one thing, Fletcher's approach is overly simplistic. Justice cannot be reduced to a trite slogan such as 'love distributed'. It is much more complex and involved than this, and is probably best regarded as a pluralistic concept. That is to say, justice cannot be reduced to a single dimension or a sole criterion.[30] Political and moral philosophers, for example, often distinguish between a number of different kinds or forms of justice. These include: (a) *social* or *distributive* justice – which is concerned with the fair or equitable allocation of resources, social goods, and political power; (b) *procedural* justice – which focuses on the need for fair, impartial procedures (e.g. a fair trial); (c) *retributive, punitive, corrective* or *criminal* justice – which is concerned with penalising those who break the law or the moral order in accordance with their deserts; and (d) *commutative* justice – which is concerned with fairness in agreements and exchanges between people (e.g. the absence of coercion or deception). Within the Catholic tradition, a further distinction is often made between social justice and distributive justice. Social justice is thought of in terms of people being able to 'participate in the creation of the common good', whereas distributive justice, as the name implies, is concerned with the fair allocation of social goods.[31]

Within the biblical tradition, the idea of justice or righteousness is connected with two Hebrew words.[32] The first, *sedaqah* (which comes from the root *tsdq*) has to do with rightness (i.e. something which is fixed and fully what it should be, or which matches up to the proper standard, or which is straight or accurate). The second, *mishpat* (which comes from the root *spt*) is concerned with concrete acts of justice or, as Wright puts it, 'with what needs to be done

in a given situation if people and circumstances are to be restored to conformity with sedaqah'.[33] Accordingly, to act justly means above all to do what is right, and this includes actions to restore and rebuild broken relationships. Note that the Hebrew concept of God's justice or righteousness is not so much a punitive or retributive justice but a *saving* or *redeeming* justice. The emphasis is on *restoring* the covenantal relationship with God and bringing *reconciliation* to the community of faith; it is more about the vindication of the righteous, the liberation of the oppressed, the forgiveness of the oppressor, and the restoration of peace or *shalom*, rather than the punishment of wrongdoers and the faithless. As Marshall puts it:

> ... biblical justice is *restorative* justice more than retributive or distributive justice. It is acting to bring about harmony and wellbeing, especially by showing concern for the disadvantaged. Thus God's justice is God's saving intervention to restore human wellbeing, to make things right.[34]

Justice is thus a complex term with a rich and varied set of meanings. It is not simply 'love distributed', as Fletcher contends. It is not simply a subset of love or another name for love. Nor is it solely about matters of distribution – although of course distributive concerns are at the heart of social justice. The requirements of justice are varied and may at times be in tension (e.g. retributive versus restorative justice). Also, whereas justice can be legislated and enforced, to enforce love is to undermine it.

But there is another problem with Fletcher's approach, namely the way he construes the nature of desert. Suppose we take justice to mean, as Aristotle argued, giving a person his or her due (*suum cuique*). This means that a person must be rewarded or punished according to his or her *deserts*. But what do people deserve? Fletcher claims that people deserve to be loved. Such an approach, however, is controversial. It can certainly be argued that the oppressed deserve liberation and that the poor and needy deserve mercy and compassion; in this sense social justice and love stand in parallel rather than in opposition. Meeting the needs of the hungry and the homeless fulfils simultaneously the requirements of mercy and social justice. But if the oppressed experience their deliverance as both an act of love and justice, for the oppressor the experience – at least in the short term – is likely to be that of judgement and retribution, even if the act is done in the spirit of love rather than vengeance. From the latter's standpoint, justice and love will be in tension, the requirements of punitive justice standing over and against those of mercy.

It is too simple to suggest, therefore, that people *deserve* to be loved. Indeed, much Christian theology has maintained the opposite: human beings, it is argued, deserve judgement not forgiveness, punishment not mercy. God's love for humanity is not based upon, or a necessary response to, our fundamental lovableness or intrinsic worth. We do not merit God's love. It is bestowed despite our utter unworthiness. It is the free, unwarranted, unexpected, and unconditional gift of grace. Furthermore, the whole notion of *loving* our neighbour implies actions which have no regard for what our neighbour actually deserves. Whether our neighbour merits our love is irrelevant. As Brunner has eloquently observed, 'love asks no questions about the nature of that which is to be loved ... loving [is] born simply of the will to love, not of the nature of the beloved. It is not a love which judges worth, but a love which bestows worth'.[35]

A further major objection to Fletcher's approach is his attempt first, to reduce the moral universe to one ethical standard (i.e. love), and second, to build into his notion of love a large number of conflicting principles or values. A central problem with this approach, as many critics have pointed out, is that love becomes so elastic that it can mean many different things. Consequently, it furnishes little, if any, specific ethical guidance. For example, suppose higher taxes will facilitate greater assistance to the needy but at the cost of a somewhat lower rate of economic growth. What is the most loving thing for a state to do? Should it give priority to the needy of today, or the wellbeing of people in the medium to longer-term? Fletcher's approach neither provides us with principles of distributive justice, nor with a capacity to weigh up the relative merits of conflicting social needs.

In sum, Fletcher misrepresents both the nature of *agape* and justice. In so doing, he wrongly equates them and misleadingly construes them as versions of the same moral imperative. It is not only Christian ethicists who find Fletcher's approach erroneous and implausible. So too do leading non-Christian scholars. To quote the eminent political philosopher John Rawls: 'The love of mankind is more comprehensive than the sense of justice and prompts acts of supererogation, whereas the latter does not'.[36]

Position 2: Love and Justice are at Times in Radical Opposition

A persistent, albeit minority, position within the history of Christian ethics, is that which sees love and justice as being, at least at times, in radical opposition to each other. When such conflicts arise, it is argued that love must prevail over justice. Such a position finds expression within certain strands of Christian Utopianism, some versions of Christian pacifism, and certain aspects of Anabaptist thought. For instance, one of the arguments advanced by some pacifists (e.g. the advocates of active, non-violent resistance to oppression or aggression) is that neighbour love cannot condone the use of lethal force, no matter how justified (from the perspective of retributive justice) such force might be. While some maintain that this prohibition on lethal force applies to Christians and non-Christians alike (and therefore by necessity to nation-states), others claim that the prohibition applies only to Christians. Either way, the requirements of love are seen as incompatible with the taking of human life, whether or not the individuals in question are deemed to be innocent. Put differently, and more theologically, those advocating such a position might claim that the eschatological and transcendent law of love can and should be *fully* actualised in this world, notwithstanding its sinfulness or fallenness; it is not necessary to wait until the parousia. To the extent that the radical command to love, as for example expressed by Jesus in the Sermon of the Mount (especially Matt. 5: 38-42), is incompatible with the requirements of power and justice, the command to love must prevail.[37]

There are, of course, many different strands of pacifism and not all of them can be located within position 2.[38] Indeed, many pacifists would vigorously reject the idea that love and justice are in radical opposition, and would defend their opposition to the use of lethal force on the grounds of both love and justice. That is to say, killing other human beings is not merely unloving, it also does nothing to further the cause of justice. In fact, it is likely to create new injustices.

Among the exponents of position 2 was the leading nineteenth century Russian novelist, and Christian Utopian, Count Leo Tolstoy.[39] According to Tolstoy, if we are to be faithful to the injunctions of Jesus, such as 'Resist not the evil one' and 'Judge not', and if we are to take seriously the commandment to love our neighbours as ourselves, then we have no alternative but to abandon the whole system of retributive justice (including the punishment of criminals, and the use of lethal force by individuals, groups or states in response to aggressive behaviour). Applied comprehensively, this position would leave little, if any, role for the state, and hence is essentially anarchistic and Utopian in nature. Needless to say, if the state lacked the right to use coercion, it could not fulfil the requirements of social justice since it would have no means to enforce the redistribution of resources.

Plainly, such a position stands in sharp contrast to the church leaders' *Social Justice Statement.* This, as noted, regards the pursuit of social justice as an integral part of our calling to love our neighbours and sees the state as the principal vehicle through which such justice is achieved.

A Brief Critique

The proposition that love and justice are fundamentally and irreconcilably opposed has no biblical warrant. To start with, it rests on a legalistic and literalistic interpretation of the Gospel accounts of some of Jesus' teaching, particularly the Sermon on the Mount. More important, it wrongly assumes that the radical requirements of neighbour love can and should be completely fulfilled in a 'fallen' world. For in a world where human evil is widespread and unabating, any attempt to sweep aside the demands of justice and to banish all forms of resistance to evil is bound to exacerbate human aggression, intensify injustice, and produce additional human suffering. Such outcomes would not be consistent with the commandment to love our neighbours. As Thielicke argues, in a world where there is no restraint on evil:

> ... it would be the weak and miserable who would get crushed. It is in order to defend them against injustice, to extend paternal love to them, that God provides the protection of force. Thus in equipping the state with punitive power ... God is actually expressing love, for in so doing he takes the weak, oppressed, and persecuted under his wing.[40]

Yet having said this, it is certainly understandable why some might conclude from the New Testament, and especially from the words of Jesus, that love and justice are at times in opposition, and that love should have priority over justice in regulating our social life. Note, for example, that some of the parables told by Jesus, such as the parable of the labourers in the vineyard and the parable of the prodigal son, appear to suggest that love and forgiveness should prevail over considerations of both social justice and retributive justice. It is interesting, too, that Jesus refused on occasions to be drawn on the application of principles of justice to particular social situations (e.g. he was unwilling to arbitrate a dispute between two brothers over the division of their family property (Luke 12:13)). Moreover, from the Gospel accounts Jesus appears to have said little about the organisation of social and political institutions, and certainly provides no detailed guidance on the proper role of the state, the appropriate form of the penal system, or the proper use of coercion and violence. In fact, some commentators have gone so far as to suggest that:

> Whereas Jesus offers us ethical principles to guide us in making our personal decisions, he seems to provide us with no principles of justice by the aid of which we may solve our social problems. He says nothing about liberty, equality, and their relations to one another, or the right distribution of goods, or the relation of the individual to society.[41]

Such a view can be challenged on many fronts.[42] Nevertheless, the point that needs to be made here is that the construction of a distinctively Christian social ethics is not without its difficulties and it is hardly surprising that the attempt to do so has generated a plethora of approaches, including those which see the radical command to love as being inconsistent with the pursuit of justice.

Position 3: Love and Justice are Different but Inseparable

The third position under consideration rejects the proposition that love and justice are identical (position 1) or at times mutually exclusive (position 2). Instead, it maintains that they are very different in nature and impose different, yet often overlapping, demands. They are nonetheless closely related to each other, if not inseparable, and ethically are equally indispensable. The views of three representatives of this position, namely Brunner, Niebuhr and Thielicke, will be outlined here. All three share in common the following convictions:

(a) Love requires justice (including both social justice and retributive justice); a failure to seek justice is thus a failure to love.
(b) Justice, although indispensable, can never be a complete or adequate expression of neighbour love; such love goes beyond or transcends justice.
(c) The realisation of both love and justice in a sinful world is fraught with difficulty; indeed, the complete fulfilment of neighbour love is impossible.
(d) Love in its 'pure', 'perfect' or 'proper' form cannot be institutionalised or applied in the public realm; it cannot be a formal part of the activity of an organisation or state; it is limited to direct I-Thou relations (although of course such relations can occur within organisations).

(e) In complex social relations or institutional contexts, love must be mediated via justice.
(f) Notwithstanding (d) and (e), to the extent that organisations and states act consistently with the demands of justice, they are in a sense giving expression to the requirements of neighbour love.

Beyond these points of agreement, however, there are some important areas of difference. For example, whereas Brunner believes that the requirements of justice can be fulfilled, Niebuhr maintains that they cannot.[43] Likewise, whereas Brunner claims that love can only do more, never less, than required by justice and that love is never in tension with justice, Niebuhr argues that love and justice have a dialectical relationship in which love, at times, stands over and against justice. Further, Niebuhr's political theology is much more positive than Thielicke's, particularly with respect to the state's role in providing social assistance.

Emil Brunner

According to Brunner, 'the nature of justice is radically different from that of love, yet ... is very closely akin to it'.[44] Broadly speaking, Brunner accepts the distinctions between love and justice as outlined in the earlier critique of Fletcher. Neighbour love is personal and involves self-giving, sacrificial behaviour; moreover, it is neither comprehensible nor rational, but 'super-rational';[45] it sets aside claims to equity in an uncalculating, risky way. Justice, by contrast, entails rendering to people their due; it is 'impersonal' and 'makes no free gift'; it is 'strictly realistic, sober and rational'.[46] Hence, whereas love is concerned for concrete persons in their uniqueness and particularity, justice is 'never concerned with the human being as such, but only with the human being in relationships. Justice belongs to the world of systems, not to the world of persons'.[47] By contrast, according to Brunner, 'love knows nought of systems'.[48] The point here, then, is that while justice is the operative principle in the public sphere (i.e. the realm of groups, organisations and states), love is the ruling principle in the personal or private sphere (e.g. the family). Yet, even in the most intimate relationships, such as marriage, justice is not entirely absent (see also Chapter 2).[49]

Brunner is not suggesting that a Christian 'must cease to be a loving human being in the world of systems'.[50] Rather, he is arguing that people can in a sense give effect to their love in groups, organisations or states by being just. In other words, people can remain loving in an institutional environment but must do so by using the currency of justice, 'since that alone is legal tender in the world of systems'.[51] Or, as he subsequently puts it, a person 'of love can only serve the state with justice'.[52] In an institutional or public context, then, love must take the form of justice. Indeed, if it does not do so, if it is applied as self-surrender, compassion or mercy it becomes mere 'sentimentality', and this, he claims, 'is the poison, the solvent which destroys all just institutions'.[53]

At the same time Brunner acknowledges that love cannot, and ought not, be banished entirely from the public sphere. As he observes, because:

> ... a member of an institution is [not] only a member of an institution, but always and only a person, there is room for love even in the most impersonal of institutions, not in the actual activity of the institution itself, but 'between the lines'.[54]

Thus, individuals can and ought to remain loving towards each other in all spheres of life, including the most impersonal or public spheres, such as the state. But love enters the public arena, not as people fulfil their 'official' roles *per se* (e.g. as a law maker, diplomat, police officer, policy adviser, teacher, administrator, etc.), but only as they express some form of discreet caring or helping, or witnessing to Christ. Correspondingly, groups, institutions and states cannot practice love as such, only justice. Love cannot, in other words, be institutionalised or take an organisational form; it is limited to direct, personal I-Thou relationships.

Nor is it appropriate for love of neighbour to be used as a benchmark for guiding the actions of groups, institutions or states. To be sure, love should motivate endeavours to reform public institutions and government policies so that they are more consistent with the requirements of God's justice. But the 'orders of creation' (such as the family and the state) should not be so transformed by love that they are no longer able to fulfil their proper function to preserve the created order (i.e. from the forces of evil and chaos). Similarly, from Brunner's perspective, it would be erroneous to regard the policies of a state as love in action – whether these policies are directed toward the end of social justice (e.g. via the provision of social assistance, education, housing or health care) or the goal of retributive justice (e.g. via the provision of courts and penal institutions). Such policies may be just, but they are not loving. For doing justice is not the same thing as loving; love only comes into play once the requirements of justice have been satisfied, supplementing them by its own free gift; for 'love transcends justice'.[55]

Importantly, Brunner argues that justice 'is always a pre-condition of love',[56] that it 'must never be neglected by love',[57] and that love must be 'perfectly just'.[58] As he puts it:

> There is therefore no such thing as love at the cost of justice or over the head of justice, but only beyond justice and through justice... . Love fulfils all the commandments of justice because it knows that its real work only begins when justice has been done.[59]

Accordingly, Brunner rejects the proposition that love may at times be in tension with justice, let alone that they might be mutually exclusive. Nor does he accept that the requirements of an official role (i.e. in an organisation or state) may prevent a person acting with love. He nonetheless accepts that whereas the obligations of justice can be fully satisfied, those of love cannot. 'Love can fulfil justice, but cannot itself be fulfilled... . Only the love which is without measure fulfils itself – the love of God'.[60]

Reinhold Niebuhr

There are close parallels between the social ethics of Brunner and Niebuhr. Like Brunner, Niebuhr argues that although love and justice are different and must rightly be distinguished, they must never be separated.[61] Christian love (*agape*), according to Niebuhr, is sacrificial, heedless, disinterested, and uncalculating. Its fullest expression is revealed in the Cross. Justice, by contrast, is discriminating and concerned with the balancing of interests and claims. Similarly, like Brunner, Niebuhr argues that love in its pure or perfect form cannot be applied directly to the public realm; rather, in complex social relations or institutional contexts love must find expression through justice. Indeed, Niebuhr maintains that in a world of pride, egoism and self-assertion the ideal of love is unobtainable (or more precisely, it is an 'impossible possibility'); such a love cannot be sustained in historical society.[62] Its wholehearted pursuit necessarily ends in tragedy, as graphically witnessed in the Cross. But while the law of love has a transcendent eschatological reference and will ultimately be fulfilled in the world to come, it is nevertheless utterly relevant to life in this world, for it provides the benchmark against which all imperfect realisations of *agape* can and must be measured and judged, both in the private and public spheres of life. Accordingly, Niebuhr rejects both naive optimism (where love is regarded as a simple possibility) and naive pessimism (where love is seen as irrelevant because it is impossible).

Pivotal to Niebuhr's approach is his view that love and justice are *dialectically* related. That is to say, they are related in both a positive and negative fashion. According to Niebuhr, a proper understanding of this dialectical relationship is fundamental to the fashioning of a coherent and genuinely Christian social ethic:

> ... the Christian conception of the relation of historical justice to the love of the Kingdom of God is a dialectical one. Love is both the fulfilment and the negation of all achievements of justice in history. Or expressed from the opposite standpoint, the achievements of justice in history may rise in indeterminate degrees to find fulfilment in a more perfect love and brotherhood; but each new level of fulfilment also contains elements which stand in contradiction to perfect love. There are therefore obligations to realise justice in indeterminate degrees but none of the realizations can assure the serenity of perfect fulfilment.[63]

Love, then, is simultaneously the fulfilment and the negation of justice. It is positively related to justice in the following ways: (a) it provides the motivation for justice, inspiring individuals to seek ever greater degrees of justice and to expose injustice; (b) it requires the pursuit of justice (for if we genuinely love others we must ensure they are justly treated); (c) it increases the potential for justice (e.g. by eliciting a reciprocal response and changing the character of human relations); (d) it enhances the manner in which justice is done (i.e. it shapes individuals' attitudes and motivations and helps ensure that justice is done in a loving, rather than judgemental, fashion); (e) it fulfils justice by transcending it (i.e. it goes beyond the precise and measured demands of justice and meets another person's very special and particular needs); and (f) it redeems justice by saving justice from degeneration. Hence, just as the Gospel fulfils and does not destroy the Law, so too love fulfils the demands of justice.

At the same time, love is negatively related to justice in that it passes judgement upon every historical realisation of justice. It stands over and against every system or form of justice (including social justice and retributive justice). Or to put it differently, love provides the ultimate perspective or standard against which the particular achievements of justice can be assessed. In so doing, it highlights the limitations and failings of all systems of justice in a sinful world. It demonstrates how they all fall short of what God requires. Equally, however, love points to ways of improvement, to the higher possibilities of justice in every situation, to the ever greater approximations of justice to itself.

Niebuhr gave considerable attention in his writing to the application of love to the public realm. In some, but by no means all, respects his views echo those of Brunner. In an organisational, group or public context, love must be changed or refracted so that justice becomes the operative principle and the appropriate goal. The main reason for this, according to Niebuhr, is that as soon as one moves beyond a relationship involving two people, in short, as soon as a third person is added, 'even the most perfect love requires a rational estimate of conflicting needs and interests'.[64] If a person has only one neighbour, the good of that neighbour can readily be given priority. If a person has more than one neighbour – as of course is the norm – judgements have to be made about which neighbour has the greatest need or is the most deserving. Complex social relations, in other words, 'require the calculation of rights' and thus considerations of justice.[65] This of course does not mean that love becomes irrelevant or inoperative. On the contrary, because of the positive relation between love and justice, the requirements of love can be at least partially fulfilled in the public realm. Consequently, he rejects the proposition that only the most personal, individual and direct expressions of social obligation are manifestations of Christian *agape*.

> Systems and principles of justice are the servants and instruments of the spirit of brotherhood in so far as they extend the sense of obligation towards the other, (a) from an immediately felt obligation, prompted by obvious need, to a continued obligation expressed in fixed principles of mutual support; (b) from the simple relation between a self and one 'other' to the complex relations of the self and the 'others'; and (c) finally from the obligations, discerned by the individual self, to the wider obligations which the community defines from its more impartial perspective.... In these three ways rules and laws of justice stand in a positive relation to the law of love.[66]

Thus, to a degree the fulfilment of the principles of justice facilitates the expression of neighbour love. As an example of this, Niebuhr points to the advantages, in terms of fulfilling the requirements of love, of having planned, organised forms of social assistance and guaranteed entitlements based on accepted social standards. As he explains:

> The unemployment benefit which the community pays to those who are out of work is partly an expression of the sense of obligation of the more privileged members of the community towards those who

> are less fortunate. They find an advantage in meeting this obligation according to fixed principles instead of relying upon their own occasional feeling of pity for this or that needy person. They know furthermore that their own knowledge of comparative needs is very inadequate and that they require the more impartial and comprehensive perspective of the total community, functioning through its proper agencies.[67]

Niebuhr acknowledges that the provision of unemployment benefits may result in particular needy individuals receiving less than they might otherwise have done by being able to appeal to a 'sensitive and opulent individual'.[68] Nevertheless, he claims that the unemployed will undoubtedly receive more via state funded (and hence coercively secured) social assistance than 'if all of them were dependent upon nothing but vagrant, momentary and capricious impulses of pity, dormant unless awakened by obvious need'.[69]

But while love and justice have a positive relation in the public sphere and with respect to the role of the state, they also have a negative relation. As Niebuhr expresses it, the systems and laws of justice

> ... contain both approximations to and contradictions of the spirit of brotherhood ... justice presupposes a tendency of various members of a community to take advantage of each other, or to be more concerned with their own weal than with that of others... . The fence and the boundary line are the symbols of the spirit of justice... . A harmony achieved through justice is therefore only an approximation to brotherhood.[70]

Moreover, the pursuit of justice in the social and political realm necessarily entails ethical tensions and pressures. Yet this does not mean we should abandon the struggle. We

> ... cannot purge ourselves of the sin and guilt in which we are involved by the moral ambiguities of politics without also disavowing responsibility for the creative possibilities of justice.[71]

And later:

> There is no escape from the paradoxical relation of history to the Kingdom of God. History moves towards the realisation of the Kingdom, but yet the judgement of God is upon every new realisation.[72]

In summary, then, for Niebuhr there is a dialectical relationship between love and justice. While justice embodies and gives expression to the calling of love, it can never fulfil the requirements of love. Love, in turn, both extends the application of justice and stands in judgement upon it.

Helmut Thielicke

Thielicke's moral and political theology has much in common with that of Brunner and Niebuhr. In particular, he rejects any notion that love and justice are utterly congruent (position 1) or mutually exclusive (position 2). At the same time his approach to the relationship between love and justice by no means parallels that of Brunner and Niebuhr.

Drawing particularly on Luther, Thielicke makes an important distinction between the 'proper work' and the 'alien work' of love.[73] The proper work of love is best exemplified and experienced in direct, personal I-Thou relationships, such as within a marriage or family, where there is genuine intimacy, gentleness, mercy, forgiveness, self-surrender and caring. By contrast, the alien work of love is that which occurs more usually within the public and institutional spheres of life. Here, according to Thielicke, 'the "manner" of love changes' and becomes evident in the 'alien work of judging, killing and repressing evil'.[74] Tillich, who takes a similar view, explains the distinction as follows:

> ... it is the alien work of love to destroy what is against love... . Love, in order to exercise its proper works, namely charity and forgiveness, must provide for a place in which this can be done, through the strange work of judging and punishing. In order to destroy what is against love, love must be united with power, and not only with power, but with compulsory power.[75]

The point here is not that the proper and alien forms of love have different spheres of validity; love is the same in all spheres of life. However, it can be expressed in two different forms, with one or other of these forms having priority depending on the context. Hence, the alien work of love is not limited to the public realm, for it is also displayed in the context of a family whenever a parent appropriately chides or disciplines a child. Likewise, the proper work of love is not limited to a family but can also be displayed within institutions. The relationship between a judge and a convicted criminal, for example, is less direct than that between a parent and a rebellious child. Nevertheless, their relationship 'is not just an objective or juridical relation, a relation of mere distance'.[76] The judge is summoned to love the criminal. This will include imposing an appropriate punishment but is not limited to this.

What of the role of the state in the area of social justice? Is the provision of social assistance via public bureaucracies the proper or alien work of love? How is the welfare state to be understood from the standpoint of love and justice? Thielicke has little to say about social justice as such, preferring to use other categories. His attitude to state-provided social assistance appears to be that it is part of the alien work of love. As such it stands, as it were, over and against, the proper work of love. Using the parable of the Good Samaritan (Luke 10: 30-37) as an illustration, Thielicke argues that the proper work of love must be personal and direct. As in the case of the Good Samaritan it has the features of immediacy, spontaneity and improvisation. He then poses the question:

> Does not the Samaritan's ministry of mercy become inconceivable, is it not altered in its very substance, the moment it is institutionalised, put in the hands of a 'Good Samaritan's League ... or even into the hands of the state itself? Is it not thereby robbed of its very point?[77]

Thielicke evidently thinks that it is. He claims that there is an inherent and unavoidable tension between love and institutionalised care,

> ... between love and advance planning, between love and purposeful intent. At its core the living claim of the Thou resists institutionalising. It cuts right across all order. It always arises as an interruption, a summons to forego all planned order ... the neighbor is an event, something that happens, a challenge, and hence something which cannot be normalised as part of an orderly scheme.[78]

From this standpoint, love of neighbour is placed at a risk, if not subverted, whenever the motive of love is expressed in an institutional form. And this danger is present whether the organisation be a Christian charity or a government social agency. After all, a night shelter run by a church organisation can be as equally bureaucratic and impersonal as the equivalent publicly-provided facility. On the whole, however, Thielicke maintains that the state is the *most* impersonal and rationalistic of institutional forms and for this reason is more likely than other organisational arrangements to place I-Thou relationships at risk.[79]

For Thielicke, then, one of the problems with organised modes of social assistance, whatever their merits in terms of social justice, is that they depersonalise human relationships and 'turn love of neighbor into a welfare machine'.[80] But he has at least three other concerns with attempts to institutionalise or rationalise love. First, as more and more caring becomes planned and organised it increasingly becomes the case that there is someone available for every case of human need. Hence, to quote Thielicke, 'no one is ever summoned personally any more. No one need feel any personal responsibility. The apparatus is available to care for everything'.[81] Second, the more comprehensive the system of organised social assistance, the fewer the opportunities for those 'who because of their faith, or because of some particular ethics, would champion personal directness in love of neighbor (as do Christians with their diaconia)'.[82] Third, whenever care of neighbour is institutionalised by Christians (especially via the state), it is not possible for it to carry a 'message that will give meaning to what is being done' (i.e. the message of the Gospel).[83]

Given these concerns, Thielicke firmly rejects the idea of a comprehensive, all-encompassing welfare state, whether democratic or totalitarian, where the state plays universal mother and father. The state must not seek a monopoly in welfare provision. It must not so extend its functions and spheres of activity that it leaves little scope for the proper work of love (i.e. the direct, spontaneous, improvised love of neighbour). On the contrary, it must actively encourage and foster voluntary initiatives, including the provision of subsidies to non-governmental groups and organisations.[84] Such a view, of course, is similar to the principle of subsidiarity in Catholic social teaching, a principle strongly endorsed in the *Social Justice Statement* (see Chapter 5).

At the same time, Thielicke utterly rejects the proposition that the persistence of hunger, illiteracy, disease and other human needs should be countenanced, if not encouraged, by the state 'in order that Christians may always have occasion for exercising a ministry of love and service'.[85] He also emphasises that the proper goal of a state's economic and social policies should be economic independence for individuals and their families. The prevention of poverty (e.g. as a result of unemployment) and the rehabilitation of the disabled or marginalised should be the *primary* policy objective, not simply the provision of direct financial assistance to those in need.

Finally, Thielicke is critical of Utopian thinking, such as

> ... the illusion that in principle poverty and helplessness can be abolished and in their stead a state of perfection attained in which human need will be completely overcome.[86]

State welfare programmes, no matter how well devised or directed, always run the risk of generating 'new forms of social pathology and new forms of poverty'.[87]

A Brief Critique

Broadly speaking, it seems to me that position 3 (as earlier summarised in points (a)-(f)) has much more to commend it than positions 1 and 2. First, it acknowledges the differences between love and justice and the complexity (if not the dialectical nature, as Niebuhr argues) of their inter-relationship. Second, it recognises that there is a difference in the *quality or form* of love which is possible in direct, personal relationships of an I-Thou variety as compared with indirect, impersonal relationships that characterise more complex social contexts. The fullest expression of *agape* is only possible in an I-Thou relationship. Third, it highlights the difficulties and tensions in applying the demands of neighbour love within the realm of groups, organisations and states. Equally, however, it acknowledges that love of neighbour is neither irrelevant to the public realm nor powerless to guide us in the design of public policy. In collective relationships love can certainly be expressed, but must take the form of justice; indeed, it cannot be made effective except by means of justice. As Thomas puts it:

> Since love of neighbor is all-inclusive, it must be given to all persons who are affected by our actions. But it cannot be given to each of the members of a large race, class, or nation directly or individually. Therefore, it must be given to them indirectly and collectively. The most effective way to do this is to seek the common good of the group by furthering justice for them.[88]

Bear in mind that neighbour love is not, as Thomas points out,

> ... primarily a sentiment or feeling: it is a practical disposition to affirm the welfare and serve the needs of others. As such, it does not depend upon a personal relationship with each of them.[89]

Fourth, position 3 maintains a proper balance between Utopianism and cynicism (or defeatism). It rejects the falsely optimistic idea that neighbour love can be fully realised in a fallen world, or – to use Thielicke's categories – that the alien work of love can cease and be superseded solely by the proper work of love. Likewise, it rejects the idea that we should abandon any attempt to fulfil the demands of *agape*. For the requirements of the Kingdom of God are not solely eschatological; they apply here and now.

But if position 3 is superior to positions 1 and 2, it is not without difficulties and objections. While the advocates of position 3 correctly emphasise the extent to which love conditions, motivates and transforms justice, they say too little about the positive impact which justice has on the way we understand and express the calling of neighbour love. Higginson, for instance, stresses that justice plays an important role in summoning love to a *breadth* and *depth* of perspective, and in giving *direction*, perhaps even *correction*, to love.[90] To illustrate, justice takes our attention away from the most eye-catching, immediate, urgent, and compelling cases of human need (e.g. the person we come across on the roadside who has been robbed and beaten) and ensures that we do not lose sight of the broader, less immediate, less observable forms of need (e.g. the people who daily face the injustices of racism, sexual harrassment, or exploitation in the workplace).

Further, an implication of position 3 is that the ideal of self-sacrifice or self-surrender has no direct application to groups, institutions or nations, only to individuals. Whereas it is proper for individuals to be willing to forgo their personal rights and to allow themselves to be insulted and imposed upon,[91] the same does not apply to groups. Yet, is there not a sense in which groups, as well as individuals, are called to practice forgiveness, to reject or at least forsake the demands of retribution, to be willing to absorb injustice, and perhaps even to engage in acts of redemptive suffering? Is it not the case even for nations that the pursuit of punitive justice should on occasions be sacrificed in the interests of reconciliation, or at least to ensure that former foes are able to re-establish a constructive and mutually beneficial relationship? I am not sure that the advocates of position 3 adequately deal with such questions.

Quite apart from this, various criticisms can be levelled at the particular theological and ethical approaches adopted by each of the three authors considered above.[92] There is not the space to deal with the full range of these here. I would, however, like to mention briefly two matters of concern.

First, the claim, especially by Brunner, that while love demands more than justice it never conflicts with justice, raises some difficult questions. Is it not the case that situations arise where there is a conflict between the requirements of mercy and forgiveness and those of retribution? Are there not situations where to be just is actually to be unloving, where love does not merely stand beyond justice but also over and against it, where love rather than transcending justice actually confronts and rejects it? Does not love often require the softening, tempering or mitigating of strict justice? Or to put it differently, is there not an inherent conflict between the proper and alien works of love?

It is not possible here to address these matters in detail. Nevertheless, it is important to note that there are at least two senses in which love can be said to *transcend* justice. On the one hand, love transcends justice when it goes *beyond* the strict demands of justice. In this situation, love involves actions which go further than what is required by considerations of duty. Love goes the extra mile, it gives above and beyond what a person needs or deserves. In so doing, however, it in no way contradicts or negates the call of justice; it simply does *more*. Social justice, for example, is likely to require a significant degree of income redistribution to ensure that the basic needs of all citizens are adequately met; if and when this goal has been achieved, its job is done. The works of love, by contrast, are never complete; they are not limited to the achievement of particular distributive outcomes. Moreover, neighbour love responds to human needs, dilemmas and tragedies with a sensitivity, empathy and compassion that transcends the capabilities of public authorities.

On the other hand, love can also be said to transcend justice when it chooses not to press the claims of justice. When a person (or nation) decides to forgive another person (or nation) a debt they owe, they are in a sense forfeiting their rightful claim. The aggrieved party could have demanded the full amount, and would have been perfectly justified in doing so. But the person (or nation) may decide instead (perhaps in the interests of reconciliation) to let the matter drop. Does this imply a breach of justice? In my view the answer is a qualified 'no'. Certainly, it means that the narrow demands of *retributive* justice have, in a sense, been set aside. But the broader demands of *restorative* or *redemptive* justice, of making things right, of restoring relationships, have not been ignored. On the contrary, they have a greater chance of being fulfilled. Of course, if the aggrieved party were forced by the offending party (or a third party) to give up their rightful claims, rather than forgiving the debt freely, this would be a different matter. In this case a new injustice would have been committed, and the former injustice would not have been put right.

Second, as argued above, Thielicke appears to be of the view that the pursuit of both social justice and retributive justice is part of the alien work of love. But while he accepts that retributive justice is necessary for facilitating the proper work of love, he argues that state activities designed to enhance social justice are in tension with the proper work of love. Institutionalised care, as best exemplified by the welfare state, not only robs love of its proper function, but also reduces the scope for genuine neighbour love. Without wishing to deny the significance of the tensions which Thielicke highlights, a number of important issues arise: Is it correct to regard the whole business of applying justice within a state, whether through the criminal justice system or welfare agencies, as an 'alien' or 'improper' work of love? And even if the concept of the 'alien work of love' is deemed to be theologically justified, is the quest for social justice to be regarded as part of the alien work of love, or is it not closer to the proper work of love (or perhaps in a different category of love altogether)? Further, is organised and planned caring necessarily contrary to the ministry of the Good Samaritan? Put differently, does the welfare state really stand over and against the Good Samaritan? Or is it not more correct, theologically speaking, to see the state as an expression of, and an instrument for fulfilling, the (proper) loving impulse of the Good Samaritan?

Haddon Willmer, in reflecting on such matters, asks what the Good Samaritan might have said in response.

> I fancy that he would have said that uncoerced neighbourliness is part of the joy of being human in God's image and fellowship. But he might say that it would also have been good to have a state which encouraged priests and levites to be more neighbourly, that discouraged the unneighbourliness of thieves, and that (since the Good Samaritan would not be on the road everyday, though people have accidents there every day) it would be good to set aside someone to be on permanent watch.[93]

Willmer goes on to suggest that through the state

> ... the Good Samaritan may be given a longer reach – the *sign* of God's love given something more of that abiding presence, that ever watchfulness, that faithfulness which are characteristic of God in his heavenly fullness... . And the Good Samaritan is the man on God's side, the man who responds to and shares in the love of God by practicing it... . The basic movement – towards others, for others, to affirm, uphold and improve their being in fellowship together – which occurs savingly in Jesus Christ ... is also fundamentally but not unambiguously characteristic of the state.[94]

Willmer's approach can certainly be questioned, but it provides a helpful corrective to Thielicke's critical attitude to state-directed care, and indeed all forms of organised social assistance. If Willmer is correct, then, despite its many and varied shortcomings, the welfare state should not be seen as being always and necessarily in opposition to the proper work of love. Rather, within certain bounds it can be a vehicle through which human beings can express their love for each other and respond to those in trouble or adversity. Indeed, in many situations it may be the only effective instrument for meeting human needs and satisfying the commandment to love. Having said this, I concur with Thielicke that it would be utterly wrong and self-defeating for the apparatus of state welfare to be so planned, comprehensive and complete that there remained no opportunities for what Wordsworth called those 'little, nameless, unremembered acts of kindness and love'.[95] It is thus vital to establish limits upon the domain of the state and ensure that it does not transgress beyond these bounds. But this is where the argument becomes difficult. What is the state's proper domain? How long should the reach of the state be in providing social assistance and responding to human need? What are the respective roles and responsibilities of individuals, families, charities and public welfare agencies? Where should the organised, systematic social provision of the state end and the generally less organised, more spontaneous caring of the family and voluntary sector begin?

The *Social Justice Statement*: A Brief Critique

It is time to return to the *Social Justice Statement* and assess its merits against the backdrop of the preceding discussion. It must be noted at the outset that such an assessment is made difficult by the brevity of the *Statement's* discussion of the relationship between love and justice. On many important matters the *Statement* is silent. Having said this, it is probably fair to argue that the *Statement* is broadly consistent with most of the central tenets of position 3 (see (a)-(f) mentioned earlier). It explicitly endorses (a) (i.e. that love requires justice), and implicitly agrees with (b) (i.e. that love goes beyond or transcends justice). It does not explicitly address (c), and indeed is open to criticism for not doing so. Nevertheless, it seems likely that the authors of the *Statement* would concur with the claim that the realisation of love and justice in a sinful world is fraught with difficulty. As far as (d) and (e) are concerned, the *Statement* is essentially silent and it is not clear what the authors would have to say about whether love can be institutionalised and whether in organisations and states love must be mediated via justice. By contrast, (f) (i.e. that organisations and states can give expression to the requirements of love) is implicitly endorsed by the *Statement*.

But if the *Statement* fits more comfortably with position 3 than positions 1 and 2, its handling of the relationship between love and justice and its discussion of the proper role of the state ignores many of the insights provided by scholars such as Brunner, Niebuhr and Thielicke (and others such as Marshall, Ramsey, Temple and Tillich who can also be placed in a roughly similar camp). Four brief criticisms can be made in this context.[96]

First, the *Statement* ignores, and in so doing implicitly rejects, the dialectical approach taken by Niebuhr. Likewise, it makes no use of Thielicke's (or more accurately Luther's) framework in distinguishing between the proper and alien works of love. The impression one is left with, therefore, is that love and justice, although different, are never in tension. Similarly, neither the *Statement* nor *Making Choices* address the problems raised by attempts to institutionalise love (e.g. via the welfare state). For example, there is no concern that state provision to satisfy the dictates of social justice may at times undermine the opportunities for private charitable initiatives and in so doing reduce the opportunities for direct neighbour love. In fact, as noted earlier, the *Statement* appears to endorse the view that the aim of public policy should be to remove the need for charity. Likewise, relatively little is said about the means by which redistribution should take place or the appropriate relations between donors (or taxpayers) and recipients (or beneficiaries).

Second, the *Statement* locates the motivation for humanity's pursuit of social justice in the love and justice of God. That is to say, we are morally obliged to seek social justice because it serves 'the loving purposes of God' (§.4) and because God is just. This approach is perfectly satisfactory so far as it goes. What is surprising, however, is that the *Statement* makes no mention of the fact that the pursuit of social justice should be part of humanity's faithful and thankful response to the love of God revealed in Christ. In other words, it is because we are loved by God that we are set free and empowered to seek the wellbeing of others, and this must include the quest for justice on their behalf.

Third, the *Statement's* handling of social justice presents some serious difficulties. Unfortunately, the *Statement* says nothing about the relationship between *social* justice and other notions or justice. Another problem lies in the claim that social justice is 'fairness'. By fairness the *Statement* means:

> ... fairness in our dealings with other people; fairness in the way responsibilities are shared; fairness in the distribution of income, wealth and power in our society; fairness in the social, economic and political structures we have created; fairness in the operation of those

> structures so that they enable all citizens to be active and productive participants in the life of society. (§.3)

Regarding social justice as 'fairness' is in keeping with much contemporary philosophical opinion, particularly that of Rawlsians. However, whether such an approach is biblically or theologically justified is another matter. Even if it is, the *Statement* provides few criteria for determining what is fair. Of the items listed in §.3, only the last (i.e. fairness in the operation of those structures so that they enable all citizens to be active and productive participants in the life of society) provides a *material* principle of justice, and even this is relatively vague. What does it mean, after all, to be an 'active' or 'productive' participant in society?

A final problem is the *Statement's* handling of the notion of 'rights'. A just order, it claims,

> ... recognises that all citizens have a right to food, housing, clothing, rest, education, health care, employment, and security in old age. Access to these things must be on the basis of need and not be limited by a person's status in society or ability to pay.

Those who reject the notion of positive rights (especially social rights) would obviously regard this formulation as flawed.[97] But even if the concept of positive rights is meaningful and morally defensible (which in my view it is), the *Statement* gives no guidance as to how the term 'right' should be understood and, in particular, what moral weight should be attached to the various rights listed. Are these rights being treated as absolute (i.e. unconditional and exceptionless) or less than absolute? Do they all carry the same moral status or do some rights have greater moral weight than others? And in the event of a clash between the rights listed, or perhaps between these and other rights (e.g. rights to property), which rights should have priority. Such matters are fundamental to the development of a clear and coherent understanding of social justice. Regrettably, the *Statement* begs more questions than it answers.

Conclusion

Christian social ethics rightly places a great deal of emphasis on love and justice. Both are central ethical imperatives. Yet how they should best be understood, how they are related, and how they should applied to the social and political realm are matters about which there is no consensus. This chapter has sought to outline some of the positions which Christians have taken over the years in their attempts to make sense of the relationship between love and justice and apply these values to the public sphere of life. I do not wish to pretend that there are any simple answers. On the contrary, love and justice are both rich and complex terms, and their inter-relationship is correspondingly complicated. Of the three positions explored in this chapter, it seems to me that position 3 (or something close to it) is the most satisfactory, certainly from a biblical perspective. In particular, I find Niebuhr's contention that there is a dialectical relationship between love and justice illuminating and persuasive. On the one hand, it rightly emphasises that love inspires us to act justly, that injustice destroys fellowship and undermines human dignity, and that love provides the conditions within which justice can be fostered and expanded – for where there is no love, how can there be justice? On the other hand, the dialectical approach acknowledges that in a sense love negates justice; it stands in judgement on all applications of the principles of justice and points to the fact that they are conditioned by, and in part a reflection of, a sinful order.

In my view, advocates of position 3 are correct in maintaining that love cannot be limited to private, direct, neighbourly acts. To love our neighbours as ourselves also requires indirect, collective and political action. If love does not seek to improve and transform the social order, if it tolerates grave structural injustices, if it ignores the needs and interests or the poor and marginalised, it is simply not being faithful to its calling. As Thomas argues, 'love is not love but sentimental talk unless it manifests itself practically in seeking justice for all'.[98] Equally, however, the pursuit of justice, though indispensable, must never be regarded as an adequate expression of neighbour love. For love transcends the requirements of justice. It must go beyond giving people what they justly deserve – whether in terms of meeting their needs or meeting out retribution. It must be willing to give sacrificially. And it must even be willing, in the interests of avoiding a gross injustice to others, to accept and absorb a gross injustice to the self.

The authors of the *Social Justice Statement* are to be commended for the emphasis which they have given to social justice, and for the way in which they locate the impulse for justice, at least in part, in the commandment to love our neighbours. As the *Statement* indicates, Christians must be concerned about the great public questions concerning the proper distribution of resources and responsibilities and the proper role of the state. Having said this, the *Statement's* handling of these questions is limited by its brevity and is open to a number criticisms. It is to be hoped that if and when New Zealand's church leaders prepare further documents in the area of social and political affairs, they will give greater attention to the complexity of the relationship between love and justice and provide a more rigorous definition of social justice.

Notes

1. E. Brunner, *Justice and the Social Order,* London: Lutterworth Press, 1945, pp. 117-8.
2. See John 3:16, 1 John 4: 7-10, Eph 1: 3-10.
3. Luke 10:27. It is useful and important to distinguish between two aspects or forms of 'neighbour love' which find expression in the New Testament. On the one hand, there is the 'Golden Rule' (Matt 7:12, Luke 6:13) and the commandment to 'love our neighbour as ourselves'. The central principle here is that we should treat others – which includes friends and enemies alike – in essentially the same way that we would like to be treated by them. On the other hand, there is the 'new commandment' that we should love one another as Christ loves us (John 13:34) and that we should love our enemies (Matt 5:44, Luke 6:35). This requires that we should go beyond the requirements of equivalence or self-interest and love unconditionally, generously and sacrificially, expecting nothing in return. For the purposes of this discussion, the focus will be primarily on the second, and more demanding, understanding of neighbour love.
4. Brunner, *Justice and the Social Order*, especially pp. 114-18; *idem*, *The Divine Imperative: A Study in Christian Ethics*, London: Lutterworth Press, 1937.
5. R. Niebuhr, *The Nature and Destiny of Man, Volume 2: Human Destiny*, London: Nisbet and Co., 1943; *idem*, *An Interpretation of Christian Ethics*, San Francisco: Harper and Row, 1963.
6. H. Thielicke, *Theological Ethics Volume 2: Politics,* Grand Rapids: Eerdmans, 1969.
7. For an analysis of the social and economic policy context in New Zealand in the early 1990s see J. Boston and P. Dalziel (eds), *The Decent Society? Essays in Response to National's Economic and Social Policies,* Auckland: Oxford University Press, 1992; C. James, *New Territory,* Wellington: Bridget Williams Books, 1993; and J. Kelsey, *Rolling Back the State,* Wellington: Bridget Williams Books, 1993.
8. There is also some material of relevance to this topic in the book which accompanied the *Social Justice Statement*. See Ruth Smithies and Helen Wilson (eds), *Making Choices: Social Justice for Our Times,* Wellington: GP Print, 1993.
9. See, for example, P. Ramsey, *Basic Christian Ethics,* Chicago: University of Chicago Press, 1950; W. Temple, *Christianity and Social Order,* London: SPCK, 1976; P. Tillich, *Love, Power and Justice,* London: Oxford University Press, 1980; J.H. Yoder, *The Christian Witness to the State,* Newton, Kansas: Faith and Life Press, 1964, esp. pp. 60-73.
10. J. Fletcher, *Situation Ethics: The New Morality,* Philadelphia, Westminster Press, 1966, p. 87.
11. Ibid., p. 88.
12. Ibid., p. 89.
13. Ibid., p. 93.
14. Ibid., p. 95.
15. Ibid., p. 87.
16. Ibid., pp. 87-88.

17. Ibid., p. 89.
18. Ibid.
19. Ibid., p. 90.
20. Ibid.
21. Ibid., p. 95.
22. Ibid.
23. J. Macquarrie, 'Justice', in J. Macquarrie (ed.), *A Dictionary of Christian Ethics,* London: SCM Press, 1984.
24. D. Forrester and D. Skene (eds), *Just Sharing: A Christian Approach to the Distribution of Wealth, Income and Benefits,* London: Epworth, 1988, p. 77.
25. Ibid., p. 79.
26. For critical analyses of Fletcher's ethical framework see, for example, N. Geisler, *Christian Ethics: Options and Issues,* Grand Rapids: Baker Book House, 1989, pp. 43-61; R. Higginson, *Dilemmas: A Christian Approach to Moral Decision Making,* Louisville: Westminster/John Knox Press, 1988, pp. 115-17.
27. Fletcher, *Situation Ethics*, p. 87.
28. See J. Burnaby, 'Love', in J. Macquarrie, *A Dictionary of Christian Ethics*, pp. 197-200; Higginson, *Dilemmas*, pp. 169-172; C.S. Lewis, *The Four Loves,* Fontana, 1963; Linda Woodhead, 'Love and Justice', *Studies in Christian Ethics*, 5/1, 1992, pp. 44-61.
29. Fletcher, *Situation Ethics*, p. 97.
30. See, for example, J. Feinberg, *Social Philosophy,* Englewood Cliffs: Prentice-Hall, 1973, pp. 98-119; K. Lebacqz, *Six Theories of Justice: Perspectives from Philosophical and Theological Ethics,* Minneapolis: Augsburg, 1986. Christian perspectives on the nature of a just society and the proper role of the state are very varied. For a range of contemporary views see: J. Chaplin (ed.), *Politics and the Parties,* Leicester: IVP, 1992; D. Forrester, *Christianity and the Future of Welfare,* London: Epworth, 1985; C. Gay, *With Liberty and Justice for Whom?,* Grand Rapids: Eerdmans, 1991; P. Marshall, *Thine is the Kingdom,* Basingstoke: Marshall, Morgan and Scott, 1984; G.S. Smith (ed.), *God and Politics,* Phillipsburg, N.J.: Presbyterian and Reformed Publishing Co., 1989.
31. K. Lebacqz, *Six Theories of Justice*, p. 73.
32. C. Wright, Living as the People of God: The Relevance of Old Testament Ethics, Leicester: IVP, 1983, pp. 133-47.
33. Ibid., p. 134.
34. C. Marshall, 'Paul's Gospel of Divine Justice', *Today's Christian*, 28, 1993, p. 32. For a fuller analysis of this approach see C. Marshall, 'Justifying Righteousness in Pauline Theology', unpublished manuscript, Bible College of New Zealand, April 1994, esp. pp. 3-13. See also D. Atkinson, *Peace in our Time,* Leicester: Inter-Varsity Press, 1985, pp. 129-36.
35. Brunner, *Justice and the Social Order*, p. 114.
36. J. Rawls, *A Theory of Justice,* Oxford: Oxford University Press, 1972, p. 192.
37. There are, of course, a range of other possible positions. For example, it might be argued that justice should be reinterpreted so that it can be brought into harmony with the requirements of love. Alternatively, it may be possible to interpret the radical demands of the Sermon on the Mount such that they are fully compatible with the requirements of justice.

38. For a range of pacifist positions see, for example, O. Barclay (ed.), *Pacifism and War,* Leicester: IVP, 1984; S. Hauerwas, *The Peaceable Kingdom,* Notre Dame: University of Notre Dame Press, 1983; J.H. Yoder, *The Politics of Jesus*, Grand Rapids: Eerdmans, 1972; *idem, Reinhold Niebuhr and Christian Pacifism,* The Church Peace Mission, Pamphlet No. 6. Scottdale: The Herald Press, 1968.
39. See, for instance, L. Tolstoy, *The Law of Love and the Law of Violence,* New York: Holt, Rinehart and Winston, 1970. For a brief examination of Tolstoy's views on love and justice see G. Thomas, *Christian Ethics and Moral Philosophy,* New York: Charles Scribner's Sons, 1955, pp. 250-51.
40. Thielicke, *Theological Ethics*, p. 243.
41. Thomas, *Christian Ethics and Moral Philosophy,* p. 247.
42. See, for example, C. Marshall, *Kingdom Come: The Kingdom of God in the Teaching of Jesus,* Auckland: Impetus Press, 1993, pp. 77-90.
43. Brunner was critical of Niebuhr's views on the nature of justice. See Lebacqz, *Six Theories of Justice*, p. 92.
44. Brunner, *Justice and the Social Order,* p. 114.
45. Ibid., p. 115.
46. Ibid.
47. Ibid., p. 116.
48. Ibid.
49. Ibid., p. 117.
50. Ibid., p. 116.
51. Ibid.
52. Ibid., p. 117.
53. Ibid.
54. Ibid, p. 117.
55. Ibid., p. 116.
56. Ibid., p. 117.
57. Ibid.
58. Ibid., p. 118.
59. Ibid.
60. Ibid., p. 118.
61. See Niebuhr, *The Nature and Destiny of Man; idem, An Interpretation of Christian Ethics*. For a critical analysis of Niebuhr's approach to the relationship between love and justice see Lebacqz, *Six Theories of Justice*, pp. 83-99. For a comparison of the views of Niebuhr and the Anglican theologian William Temple, see A. Suggate, *William Temple and Christian Social Ethics Today,* Edinburgh: T and T Clark, 1987.
62. See Niebuhr, *An Interpretation of Christian Ethics,* pp. 62-83.
63. Niebuhr, *The Nature and Destiny of Man*, p. 255.
64. Ibid., p. 257.
65. Ibid., p. 261. As Atkinson puts it: 'We can understand what is meant by 'love your neighbour' when we think of our neighbours one by one in terms of single relationships. But what can 'love your neighbour' mean in national terms? It means that we must seek to express our love for all our neighbours by facilitating justice. Likewise, love for enemies in national and social terms can be expressed in the quest for justice in our dealings with them, and for the vindication of justice in our conflicts with them', *Peace in Our Time*, p. 136.

66. Niebuhr, *The Nature and Destiny of Man*, p. 257.
67. Ibid., p. 259.
68. Ibid., p. 260.
69. Ibid.
70. Ibid., p. 261.
71. Ibid., p. 294.
72. Ibid., p. 296.
73. Thielicke, *Theological Ethics*, p. 243.
74. Ibid.
75. Tillich, *Love, Power and Justice*, pp. 49-50.
76 Thielicke, *Theological Ethics*, p. 244.
77. Ibid., p. 291.
78. Ibid.
79. Ibid., p. 309.
80. Ibid., p. 291.
81. Ibid., p. 292.
82. Ibid.
83. Ibid., p. 290.
84. Ibid., p. 308.
85. Ibid., p. 306.
86. Ibid., p. 310.
87. Ibid.
88. Thomas, *Christian Ethics and Moral Philosophy*, p. 254.
89. Ibid., p. 255.
90. Higginson, *Dilemmas*, pp. 178-184.
91. See Matt. 5:39.
92. For a critique of Brunner, see H. Dooyeweerd, *A New Critique of Theoretical Thought, Volume 1*. Amsterdam: Presbyterian and Reformed, 1953, pp. 519-21. For critiques of Niebuhr, see Hauerwas, *The Peaceable Kingdom*, pp. 135-42; Higginson, *Dilemmas*, pp. 106-11; Lebacqz, *Six Theories of Justice*, pp. 83-99; and Yoder, *Reinhold Niebuhr and Christian Pacifism.* For a critique of Thielicke see O. O'Donovan, *Resurrection and Moral Order,* Leicester: IVP, 1986, pp. 144-46.
93. H. Willmer, 'Towards a Theology of the State' in D. Wright (ed.), *Essays in Evangelical Social Ethics,* Leicester: IVP, 1983, p. 95.
94. Ibid., p. 95.
95. W. Wordsworth, 'Lines composed a few miles above Tintern Abbey'.
96. For a critical analysis of my concerns about the *Social Justice Statement* in an earlier version of this chapter, see Ann Wansbrough, 'Making a Difference: What can the Australian Churches Learn from the New Zealand Heads of Churches 1993 Programme: *Making Choices: Social Justice for our Times*', Board for Social Responsibility, Uniting Church of Australia, NSW Synod.
97. See, for example, R. Nozick, *Anarchy, State and Utopia,* Oxford: Basil Blackwell, 1974. For a defense of the concept of positive rights see J. Boston, 'Is Social Democracy Morally Defensible?' in *Reshaping Social Democracy,* Gamma Occasional Papers, No. 4, Wellington, 1993, pp. 47-64; R. Plant, 'Citizenship, Rights and Welfare' in A.

Coote (ed.), *The Welfare of Citizens: Developing New Social Rights,* London: Institute for Public Policy Research, 1992. Whether or not the concept of positive rights can be defended philosophically, it is worth noting that liberals on both the 'left' and the 'right' have a tendency to absolutise individuals and their rights, while at the same time ignoring their responsibilities and the demands of God upon humanity.

98. Thomas, *Christian Ethics and Moral Philosophy*, p. 256.

Chapter 4

The Use of the Bible in Ethics

Scripture, Ethics and the Social Justice Statement

Christopher Marshall

Introduction

The church leaders' *Social Justice Statement* is an impressive exercise in ecumenical collaboration and Christian social responsibility. That leaders of ten different denominations could jointly produce such a document, and arrange to have it read in churches throughout the land, is no small achievement. Although the *Statement* has been criticised by politicians and journalists for being short on specific policy recommendations, and hence simplistic, and by some church people for being partisan in its political and economic stance, it represents a laudable attempt by the Christian community to make serious social comment on some of the disturbing developments in our recent social and economic life.

The framers of the *Social Justice Statement* believe that the views expressed in the document flow directly from the Christian gospel and are consistent with 'the values taught in the Scriptures' (§.1) and 'the teaching of Jesus Christ and the Hebrew Scriptures' (§.6). There is, however, only a limited attempt to justify this by explicit appeal to the Bible. There are some Bible citations in the *Statement*,[1] but it would appear that the Christian leaders have sought 'middle axioms' through which to express Christian values in terms intelligible to the wider secular community (see Chapter 1).[2] An examination of the associated study book, *Making Choices: Social Justice for Our Times,* intended for use in churches, reveals a different picture. Here there is considerable reference to biblical teaching. The declared purpose of the book is to help Christians 'reflect on the moral teaching drawn from the Bible and apply it to the reality of life in New Zealand society'.[3] The hope, no doubt, is for a repeat of the apostle Paul's Beroean experience, where the synagogue congregation 'welcomed the message very eagerly and examined the Scriptures every day to see whether these things were so' (Ac 17:11).

This, too, is commendable. It presupposes that ordinary church-goers are not only interested in studying the Bible but consider it crucial that Christian moral and social values be consistent with those of the Bible. For those of us who earn a living from promoting knowledge of the Bible this is very reassuring, especially in these days of redundancy and economic constraint! Although the level of biblical literacy in our churches continues to decline, and the extent of engagement with the biblical text in most Sunday sermons is very limited, there remains an instinctive feeling that the Bible is important, and that even the declarations of bishops, cardinals, moderators and general secretaries need ultimately to be tested against Holy Writ.

In this chapter I wish to think a little more about how the Scriptures can function in Christian ethical reflection. Much of what I say may seem self-evident, and it really only provides a partial prolegomenon to the actual task of articulating a social ethic deeply conditioned by the biblical witness. Space and circumstances, not to mention limited competence, prevent me from addressing the latter here.

Sources of Ethical Guidance

1. The Components of Christian Ethics

For the purposes of this discussion, ethics may be understood as the systematic study of the moral principles, values and obligations that guide human behaviour. While 'morality' concerns the *evaluation* of such behaviour as right or wrong, good or bad, 'ethics' is the *theoretical analysis* of the major ingredients that shape and validate these moral judgements.[4] 'Christian' ethics is the attempt to understand and justify moral obligation in relation to the will of God, the Creator, Redeemer and Sustainer of all. This makes Christian ethics a distinctive enterprise.[5] That is not to say that the *content* of Christian moral values is radically different from the content of non-Christian values. There are important differences,[6] but Christian attitudes to what is right and wrong are often widely shared by non-Christians. The distinctiveness of Christian ethics lies primarily in the way Christians understand the ultimate origin and sanction of these values. At the heart of Christian ethics lies an appeal to *revelation.* Christian ethical judgements are governed ultimately by belief in the self-disclosure of God's own moral character and will, pre-eminently in the person and work of Jesus Christ, not by the dictates of human reason, affections, volition or environmental conditioning.

In the attempt to clarify the ethical corollaries of divine revelation, Christian ethics draws on five main sources of guidance.

(a) *Scripture:* The Bible serves as the primary record of God's self-disclosure in the events of salvation-history, as apprehended by the community of faith. Inasmuch as it presents God as a righteous Being who demands righteousness of his creatures, the Bible is profoundly concerned with ethics. According to biblical tradition, ethical behaviour stands in a two-fold relationship to God's self-revelation. On the one hand, it is a *response of gratitude* for God's saving acts in history, while on the other hand, those saving acts themselves provide the *pattern and standard* for human conduct. The people of God are enjoined to model their behaviour on the actions of God; the covenant requires nothing less that the 'imitation of God' (Lev 11:45). The meaning of 'justice', for instance, is arrived at not by contemplating some abstract norm of justice, but by remembering how God delivered his people from oppression, and then acting accordingly.[7] For Christian ethics, the imitation of God centres on the imitation of Christ (1 Pet 2:21), whose concrete manner of living and acting is known to us only through the biblical record.[8]

(b) *Theological Tradition:* Revelation, including biblical revelation, is received, reflected on, and interpreted by the people of God, down through history. This interpretation and application of revelation constitutes the theological and moral tradition of Christianity, which serves as a second source for discerning God's will. It is not only the Catholic Church that so uses tradition; all branches of Christianity have appealed to historical precedents and experience in formulating moral and doctrinal teaching. Such tradition is more than a collection of dogmatic and moral propositions transmitted from the past; it is also the 'story' of a particular people, handed on and reappropriated by each generation. We cannot separate ourselves from our traditions and heritage. We enter into life in the midst of tradition; we are fundamentally shaped by tradition; and even our ability to question and change tradition comes from the tradition itself.

(c) *Moral Philosophy:* The great moral traditions of Western philosophy, which have appealed principally to the exercise of human reason for the determination of right and wrong, have also had a profound impact on both the content and methodology of Christian ethics (the very word 'ethics' is the legacy of Greek philosophy). Of particular significance has been the concept of natural law, which has been very influential in Catholic moral theology. The extent to which natural law considerations should shape Christian ethics is much contested, but some concept of a 'natural' revelation of God's moral will accessible to all humanity in virtue of creation has played a role in most expressions of Christian ethics, including New Testament ethics (e.g. Matt 5:46f; Rom 1:28; 2:14ff; Ac 17:16-34; 1 Cor 11:13ff).[9]

(d) *Empirical Data:* Christian ethics is more than a speculative exercise; it also requires attention to the full range of contextual factors that bear on each ethical situation. Indeed, the first task of moral analysis is to clarify the decision-making situation and identify the range of available options. The data furnished by the social sciences and by other empirical analyses thus has an indispensable role in ethical discernment. The special contribution of such descriptive research is to keep ethical evaluation in touch with reality, where the rubber hits the road.[10]

(e) *The Spirit-in-Community*: The New Testament places great emphasis on a two-fold role for the Holy Spirit in Christian ethical life – that of bringing about inner moral renewal in believers so that they spontaneously manifest ethical virtues,[11] and of guiding them in ethical decision-making.[12] Moral character-formation and moral decision-making are inseparably linked within the Spirit's orbit. It is crucial to recognise that in the New Testament the Spirit's work is expressed in the context of the church.[13] 'Paul knows nothing of solitary religion or individual morality', explains W.D. Davies, 'but rather sees the Christian firmly based in the community'.[14] The gathered community provides the necessary checks and balances which prevent the Spirit's direction degenerating into individualistic subjectivism.

This list of the main sources of Christian ethics invites two immediate observations. The first is that while the five components may be conceptually distinguished, they are in practice inseparable. Scripture cannot be entirely distinguished from tradition, since Scripture is both the product of tradition and the shaper of tradition. Empirical data does not exist in isolation from the moral values and ideological commitments that govern the gathering, classification and interpretation of data (a point not to be overlooked in the current economic environment). The Spirit's guidance of the community is not merely intuitive but often employs the text of Scripture and the wisdom learned from ecclesiastical tradition or scientific discovery.[15] The five sources, then, are intertwined. Yet there is still value in distinguishing them, for in different Christian traditions different constituents have the dominant role, although in all traditions ethical arguments gain in persuasiveness by employing all five in a coherent way.

Second, our delineation of several sources of ethical guidance shows that the catch-cry *sola Scriptura* does not really apply in Christian ethics. 'Scripture *alone*', contends Gustafson, 'is never the final court of appeal for Christian ethics'.[16] By itself the Bible is not enough to tell us what to do. The Bible may be a necessary source for Christian ethical reflection, but it is not a sufficient resource on its own. Arriving at moral judgements entails a dialectic between scriptural and non-scriptural factors, between considerations based on circumstance and rational inquiry and those which appeal to the biblical witness. The challenge of Christian ethics is to achieve a judicious balance between these considerations in the task of moral deliberation. The *Social Justice Statement* is itself evidence of such an attempt. Alongside Scripture, reference is made to the tradition of the church, the Treaty of Waitangi, political philosophy, and socioeconomic trends. Such a dialogical interplay between Scripture and experience is unavoidable, for every claim to understand the Bible presupposes finite human interpretation, and every interpretation is invariably conditioned by a wide range of (extra-biblical) personal and contextual factors.

Having said that, for most Christians, including those who do not subscribe to a 'high' doctrine of biblical inspiration, Scripture is still felt to possess a unique authority in Christian ethical reasoning. The essential test of validity for ethical judgements is whether they are consistent with what is perceived to be scriptural teaching. Even if our understanding of that teaching is subject to change, Scripture *per se* has long been accorded, at least in theory,[17] a privileged role in adjudicating Christian moral teaching; indeed it is precisely as an authority that the Bible has chiefly been employed in Christian ethics.[18]

2. *The Role of Scripture*

Much has happened over the past 200 years to undermine the privileged position traditionally accorded Scripture in determining Christian thought and practice. For many interpreters today, such considerations as the pre-scientific world-view of the biblical authors, their reliance upon primitive mythological language and apocalyptic symbolism, the alleged dependence of New Testament ethics on a discredited imminent eschatology,[19] and the sheer, irreconcilable diversity of ethical perspectives in Scripture, make it impossible to ascribe a normative role to the Bible in ethical deliberations.[20] And yet, as Marshall observes, 'there remains a lingering suspicion that the Bible *is* authoritative; sermons are still based on biblical texts, and if a preacher or scholar disagrees with what Scripture says, he usually feels compelled to produce some good reasons for his disagreement'.[21] Whatever the problems in appropriating Scripture today – and they are considerable – there continues to be a widespread conviction, across confessional lines, that Scripture can, does, and should shape Christian moral life. And there remain strong historical, theological and practical arguments for according the Bible such a decisive or normative role.

Historically, the Bible has significantly shaped the moral ethos of Western culture. In the past, considerable knowledge of the Bible was transmitted through general culture, and biblical authority was almost universally accepted in the West. This is no longer the case, so that comparison with the Bible provides one yardstick for measuring changes in the moral values of contemporary society. Such a comparison is evident in the *Social Justice Statement.* Recent developments in social and economic policy are identified in the *Statement* as departures both from biblical teaching (§§. 1, 2, 6, etc.) and from values previously cherished in New Zealand society (e.g. §§. 33, 39, 43, 45, 47). This highlights the declining power of the Judaeo-Christian ethic in shaping our social and cultural life.

Theologically, the Christian community still affirms, with a fair measure of confidence, that the Bible contains or bears witness to divine revelation. Most important in this respect is the fact that it provides our only access to God's self-disclosure in the life, death and resurrection of Christ, to whom Christians are directly accountable. In the final analysis, it is because Christian believers discover themselves to be directly encountered by Christ in the text of Scripture that they continue to listen to Scripture.

Practically, the Bible provides an indispensable framework for understanding the human situation in general, and the task of the Christian community in particular. The biblical story offers a perspective on the human condition that carries the conviction of truth. It attests, as Gustafson observes, both to the limitations and the potentialities of human action in the world.[22] It affirms the existence of moral evil; the temptations to pride and arrogance in human achievements; the capacity for people to rationalise destructive behaviour by appealing to noble ends; the finitude of moral judgements. It provides, on the other hand, a vision of the possibilities of human life. It affirms that the unfulfilled future is in the hands of a compassionate and just God; it gives insight into God's ultimate intentions in history; it describes actions and events that are seen to be consistent or inconsistent with God's aspirations for humanity; it gives voice to the longing of oppressed people for peace and justice; and it depicts the creation of a special people to serve as co-workers with God in bringing these about. All this has profound ethical significance.

> This scriptural faith disposes the Christian community toward moral seriousness, toward profound dissatisfaction with those events that are destructive of human life and value, toward aspirations for a future which is more fulfilling for all God's creation; and thus toward negative judgement on events which are not consistent with the possibilities that God is creating for man.[23]

Thus, while Scripture is not, and cannot, be an exclusive source of guidance for Christian ethics (even within the New Testament written Scripture does not fulfil such an exclusive role),[24] there is good reason to regard it as the *primary* or *normative* authority for Christian morality and identity. And, as George Lindbeck notes, the 'instinct of the faithful' is still to invest such worth in Scripture, even if popular knowledge of the actual content of Scripture is in noticeable decline, inside as well as outside the church.[25] Despite this, the Christian community is still more ready to accept ethical judgements that run counter to theological tradition or philosophical morality or contemporary scientific judgement or the advice of their clerical leaders than those that are plainly inconsistent with Scripture.

But none of this takes us very far. It is one thing to assert the unique authority of Scripture for Christian morality; it is quite another to demonstrate *how* the Scriptures can most appropriately function this way, and to decide precisely *what* Scripture authorises and denies. The fundamental issue is not *whether* the Bible is authoritative for ethics but *how* we move from biblical ethical judgements to present problems. Using an ancient religious text, even an inspired one, for ethical guidance today is fraught with hermeneutical difficulties, and the Bible itself does not give us clear instructions on how to reason from its moral imperatives to their practical application to the problems of real life. Consequently ways of interpreting both the ethics of Scripture, and the use of Scripture in ethics, vary enormously.[26]

3. *Some Hermeneutical Problems*

A great deal could be said about the hermeneutical hurdles that confront the Christian ethicist in turning to Scripture.[27] The most obvious is the problem of *historical distance,* the fact that we face ethical dilemmas today of which the Bible knows nothing. How can the Bible be a lamp for our feet in matters such as genetic engineering, *in-vitro* fertilisation, nuclear weapons, world hunger, or free-market economics? Even in areas of current concern to which the Bible does apparently speak (e.g. politics, war, labour relations, marriage and sexuality), it presupposes a radically different socio-political reality, with a different range of options open to actors. How can advice given in one context be reapplied in another, totally different context, even if the topic under discussion is the same? Just because the topic is the same does not mean the central issues are the same.

Now the problems of historical distance are certainly weighty; to disregard them is to doom the Scriptures to irrelevance. But the dilemma is perhaps not as serious as some allege,[28] since the most pressing ethical issues human beings face, even those peculiar to modern life, usually turn on perennial questions of power, wealth, violence, class or gender, and about such matters the Bible speaks extensively.[29] Although the Bible cannot function as a direct guide with respect to many modern problems, particular courses of action can still be evaluated in light of the central commitments of the biblical text on matters of power, wealth, justice and the like.

More serious than the problem of cultural distance is the many-sided phenomenon of *pluralism* that confronts us in the interpretation of Scripture. There is, first, the pluralism in the *content and expression of biblical morality itself.* There is no shortage of ethical material in Scripture. But it comes in a huge diversity of literary forms – commands, laws, warnings, exhortations, prohibitions, wisdom teaching, proverbs, allegories, prayers, parables, visions of the future, narratives, living examples, dialogues, vice and virtue lists, and more. Different forms of moral discourse require different modes of interpretation. More than this, there is diversity in the ethical perspectives presented on particular themes, such as the handling of wealth. In some places, the biblical writers endorse a prudential morality accessible to everyone; in other places, they propose an ethical absolutism that defies every canon of common sense or social pragmatism.[30] As the record of God's interaction with people over a long historical period, and in a wide range of cultural and social situations, there is *development* as well as variety in biblical ethics. Scripture is an historical document, not a legal constitution in which all parts can be treated as equally important for all generations. There is both intracanonical *dialogue,* with one part of Scripture interpreting and complementing another; and intracanonical *critique*, with some perspectives being relegated to preparatory and accommodating roles.[31]

Now the sheer quantity, variety and historical conditionedness of ethical material in the Bible makes sustaining any 'objective' authority for Scripture problematic. It poses the question of how we do justice to the variety of perspectives Scripture offers without imposing our own agenda. How do we determine the continuities and moral priorities of Scripture? How do we bring some degree of organisation and integration to biblical teaching? Is such secondary organisation legitimate, or is it an arbitrary imposition on a heterogeneous range of texts? Is it admissible to set up a canon within a canon? Can we in fact avoid doing so?[32]

Such internal canonical pluralism is matched, second, by a pluralism of *historical and theological reconstructions* of the biblical message. There has always been a diversity of ways of construing the overall unity of biblical teaching – be it in terms of covenant, nature and grace, law and gospel, sequential dispensations, the Kingdom of God, and so on. To this diversity has been added the results of modern historical criticism. Invaluable light has been shed on the biblical world by historical criticism, but it has also spawned an enormous diversity of explanations for the origin and meaning of the text, all of which are tentative and constantly changing. One result of historical criticism has been to convince the educated laity that biblical interpretation is a technical enterprise that requires prolonged specialised training, so that 'it is now the scholarly rather than the hierarchical clerical élite which holds the Bible captive and makes it inaccessible to ordinary folk'.[33]

Third, there is a pluralism of *modern idioms and conceptions* that the biblical message is translated into, some philosophical, some political, some mystical. How do we decide what is, and what is not, a faithful reinterpretation of the biblical message? The conscious attempt of modern interpreters to re-express biblical thought in the language of the day, while both helpful and necessary, has resulted in a 'pluralistic cacophony' of diverse and variable accounts that are often mutually unintelligible.[34] Indeed, such is the diversity of modern approaches to biblical interpretation that it has become increasingly problematic to speak of the 'meaning' of the text at all. For a text can mean different things to different people, depending on the interpretive interests pursued by the reader, and there is no impartial way of determining the text's 'real' or 'true' meaning.[35]

Modern (more so post-modern) readers of Scripture are more aware than ever before in history of the hermeneutical dilemmas posed by this three-fold pluralism. Sadly, for many ordinary Christians the Bible has become a closed book. Yet there is no magical way of avoiding such pluralism. The problem exists, it is real, and it has to be faced whenever we turn to Scripture for guidance in ethical decisions. What Richard Hays calls 'bumper sticker hermeneutics' – 'God said it, I believe it, that settles it' – is clearly no solution, since it ignores rather than solves the problem.[36]

But the alternative need not be total relativism or scepticism. Written texts always retain a certain independence of voice over against those of their interpreters, a capacity to challenge readings based on inappropriate or alien assumptions. If this is true of texts in general, it is even more true of Scripture, which, Christians confess, is used by the Spirit-in-community to convey the mind of God to God's people. As long as we are prepared to consent to biblical authority, to be self-critical of our own handling of the text, to allow Scripture to be a 'two-edged sword' that can challenge our presuppositions and expose the interpretive filters of our social location, and be open to the possibility, even the necessity, of diverse yet equally faithful appropriations of the text today, the hermeneutical problems of using Scripture for ethics are not insuperable.

4. The Search for a Method

If then the Bible *should*, and, despite the above hurdles, *can* be used as a normative reference point in ethical decision-making, it seems self-evident that a method must be devised for exploring the moral implications of Scripture in a systematic and not in a haphazard way.[37] Most biblical interpreters have agreed on this for a long time. Yet despite their very best efforts, none have succeeded in devising a comprehensive method for moving from the text of Scripture to the current situation.[38]

In view of this, there is a growing recognition that the quest for a single definitive method is misguided. It is misguided for at least two reasons. The first is that no single method can cope with the pluriformity of Scripture itself. Since there is a variety of materials in Scripture, there needs to be a variety of ways of construing its moral application. 'To reduce Scripture's moral requirements to any single category is to distort both morality and Scripture'.[39] Second, there is no one method that can straddle the diversity of contemporary contexts readers find themselves in. Fowl and Jones argue that past attempts to specify a clear and precise method have rested on the false assumption that ethical decisions are made by isolated individuals, who ought to follow a rationally-defensible method, the validity of which is independent of social and historical circumstances. But individuals learn to make moral judgements in particular historical communities; moral descriptions employ the categories and commitments of distinct social traditions; and even if it were possible to identify generalisable methodological principles, every attempt to apply them is context-dependent. Accordingly, 'the search for a context-independent method is bound to fail'.[40]

This is not to deny the value of systematic methodological reflection, nor to advocate a complete relativism where every interpretation is equally valid. It is simply to recognise the *variety* of ways Scripture can be used in ethics, and to insist that there is no neutral, transcendent, fail-safe method for evaluating specific appropriations of the text. Moral reasoning and justification are still of critical importance, but such evaluations can only be made by particular communities in particular situations, under the guidance of the Spirit and drawing on all the resources available to them at the time. These resources will include methodological controls appropriate to the character and vision of the community.

Various typologies have been suggested to describe how the Scriptures have been used in ethics. In what follows, I will employ a tripartite classification, with various sub-categories. It must be stressed that these categories are not distinct, mutually exclusive methods pursued in opposition to each other; in practice most biblical scholars and ethicists blend elements of all three (although often with one or other occupying the driving seat). It is not my intention to suggest that the three broad approaches form a methodological hierarchy, with the third approach superseding the earlier two. Each method has a valid and irreducible contribution to make. Therefore, after analysing the strengths and weaknesses inherent in each way of using Scripture, we will reaffirm the merits of a methodological pluralism. But there is still value in teasing out the different assumptions and priorities at work in each distinct way of employing Scripture in ethics so that we have some basis for understanding competing evaluations of the moral witness of Scripture in particular issues, such as those addressed in the *Social Justice Statement*.

The Prescriptive Use of Scripture

In this method the Bible is understood as *prescribing* moral rules, ordinances, commands, principles or ideals, which are to be faithfully observed in current situations. This approach has a very long history[41] and is perhaps still the most common way the ethical authority of the Bible is understood by Christians. The prescriptive use gives maximum value to the sizeable collections of moral imperatives in the Bible – the laws of the Pentateuch, the moral precepts of Proverbs, the criticisms of the prophets, the ethical teaching of Jesus, the moral codes of the epistles. Together these constitute a 'revealed morality' that demands obedience; deontological reasoning prevails over teleological or consequentialist considerations.[42] There are two main expressions of the prescriptive use of the Bible, though each has many possible permutations.

1. Biblical Moralism

One expression is a straightforward *biblicism* which treats the Bible as a rule book and insists on literalistic adherence to the letter of the law. Actions are deemed morally wrong if they violate the rules and regulations specified in any of the biblical texts, and morally right if some explicit biblical warrant, contrived or otherwise, can be cited. The merit of this approach is the attention it gives to the numerous divine imperatives and sanctions in the biblical text, and to some New Testament depictions of Jesus as, in some sense, a new Lawgiver (e.g. by Matthew). But there are also severe methodological flaws in the approach.

(a) It is *inherently selective* in the way it uses the biblical evidence; it accepts as binding certain imperatives and not others.[43] There is a pre-understanding at work that governs the choice of texts to be applied to particular situations and that provides ways of explaining away other texts that would, on the surface of it, contravene the moral stance being adopted. The diversity of biblical ethical teaching is reduced to a predetermined uniformity.
(b) Advocates of this approach are often guilty of *inadequate exegesis.* They tend to gloss over the exegetical difficulties tied up with appeals to particular texts and assume that their application today is relatively straightforward. They also fail to take the historical character of biblical teaching seriously, wherein certain moral prescriptions are rendered obsolete by later developments. Instead the Bible is treated as a flat-text, with each part potentially carrying the same moral authority today as any other. As Birch and Rasmussen warn:

> The church must constantly guard against those who would declare moral imperatives in areas where the biblical witness does not warrant this. The history of the church is filled with examples of those who endow some limited portion of Scripture with absolute moral authority. Careful exegesis in the context of the entire canon is a safeguard ... . Only those concerns consistently identified throughout Scripture as moral imperatives necessary to the authentic self-understanding of God's people can be claimed as necessary marks of faith on biblical grounds.[44]

(c) There is a tendency to *legalism or superstition*. The paradigm of 'law' governs interpretation of ethics in general, so that the words of Jesus or Paul are taken, at least in intent,[45] as legal prescriptions in the same way as Old Testament commands. Emphasis falls on external conformity to pre-set rules, with little attention being paid to the motivations, intentions or consequences of ethical decisions. As a result, obedience to biblical injunctions ceases to be genuinely moral, since moral decision-making requires a free choosing of the good in light of particular circumstances, not a mechanical adherence to rules. Human morality is too complex to define simply in terms of adhering to a law code.

(d) In treating the Bible as a source of moral rules, the method distorts *the kind of book the Bible is*. Certainly the Bible includes laws and imperatives. But such material constitutes a very small proportion of the total text; the dominant literary genre is *narrative,* not law.[46] This is even the case in the Pentateuch, where most of the legal material of the Old Testament is found. Even in interpreting the legal and moral prescriptions, it needs to be recognised that they were never formulated as timeless truths but as timely applications of God's will in specific situations. The very fact that they were intended to be relevant to *that* situation implies they are not *directly* applicable to *our* situation.[47] To treat all biblical prescriptions as eternally valid rules of conduct begs the question of the intention behind their original formulation.

(e) Direct enforcement of biblical injunctions regardless of circumstances can end up with *ethical results* out of harmony with the spirit of biblical teaching or the moral wisdom of the church's tradition. The logic of this position is either a reversal of cultural development and a freezing of life in a past age, or the elaboration of an accompanying body of oral or written interpretations to apply the laws to changing situations, such as found in Rabbinic Judaism.[48] Neither option has been generally adopted by the church.

(f) Finally, biblical moralism works best in matters of personal morality, but has little to offer *Christian social ethics*, since the New Testament has little in the way of explicit social legislation.[49] It may be possible to govern one's personal conduct according to a check-list of biblical prescriptions; it is impossible to organise complex social interrelationships, which invariably entail conflict and the need for compromise, on such a basis.

2. *Biblical Casuistry*

The other main expression of the prescriptive approach is a more sophisticated *casuistry* that seeks to discern underlying principles and ideals behind biblical teaching, then reapply them in contemporary situations. This method overcomes the problems of biblicism by positing a distinction between two main forms of ethical guidance (though the terminology used to identify each varies).[50] On the one hand there are *ethical directives,* specific ethical instructions or rules that summons obedience to particular demands. The key thing about such directives is that they are addressed to, and are to be obeyed within, a specific cultural setting. Rules do not make sense in a cultural vacuum. On the other hand there are *ethical principles,* general statements of conduct that do not tell us what to do in detail but point us in a particular direction or advocate a particular quality of conduct. Such principles or ideals are trans-situational; once identified they can be applied authoritatively in a variety of contexts. Sometimes these moral or theological principles are stated explicitly in the text;[51] at other times they lie buried beneath specific teaching or narrative and need to be excavated.[52] The supreme norm, around which all such principles orbit, is that of Christ-like love: 'love one another as I have loved you' (Jn 14:15).

Thus, the job of Christian ethics is to extract fundamental ethical principles from Scripture, then find culturally-appropriate ways (or binding prescriptions) to translate these principles into our situation. 'The task of the biblical moralist', says Marshall, 'is to extrapolate from Scripture to the particular ethical exhortations appropriate in different situations'.[53] Such applications will vary from place to place and time to time. Consequently, the task of deriving new rules from old principles is an on-going one. Both sides of this ethical task are important. If we simply stress ethical rules in Scripture, we end up in rigid legalism. If we stop at the level of identifying general principles without granting specific application, (e.g. 'do what love requires in each unique situation'), we end up in total subjectivism.

Now this method of using Scripture for ethics has several strengths.

(a) It takes *biblical authority* seriously; all biblical teaching, not just specific ethical injunctions, is treated with respect, since ethical principles relevant to some contemporary situation may be locked up in material that at first sight has little resemblance to the modern problem. Even the sternest, most uncompromising demands, such as the 'hard sayings' of Jesus, can receive a genuine hearing when one is searching for underlying ideals and principles.

(b) We are not forced to take literally commands which are no longer applicable in changed circumstances. Instead of a wooden literalism, we are free to find *creative re-applications* of underlying principles, without minimising the importance of concrete prescriptions. Our task is to follow the biblical message faithfully rather than literally.

(c) It enables us to cope better with *diversity* in biblical morality. The existence of such diversity is explained by the fact that the same principles may find quite different expressions in different situations. Conversely, the extant variety of concrete ethical advice in Scripture all but requires some attempt to discern guiding convictions behind it.

(d) When the norm of *agape* is given a governing role, as it is in the New Testament itself, *harsh legalism is ruled out.* For love, by its very nature, requires that situational factors are taken into account in applying biblical teaching, so that in a given instance it may be the most loving application of a principle to do the very opposite of a specific biblical injunction (e.g. refusing to give freely to an alcoholic [cf. Lk 6:30], or to pay taxes where they will be used to prepare for nuclear genocide [cf. Rom 13:6]).

(e) It allows for *continuing progress* in ethical application beyond the canonical boundaries.[54] Slavery is tolerated in the Bible, but there are other principles in biblical morality that ultimately render it unacceptable. Patriarchy is presupposed in biblical teaching, but the principle of equality, enunciated most clearly in Gal 3:28, heralds its eventual transcendence, while subverting its oppressive character in the meantime. Capital punishment is explicitly sanctioned in the Old Testament and challenged only by implication in the New. But there was good reason to make the implied challenge explicit at a subsequent period, in light of the broader concerns of the gospel.

The positive features of this casuistic approach are therefore considerable. But the method is also open to abuse and criticism.

(a) It can easily become too *rationalistic and abstract.* It begins with concrete examples, then moves up the ladder of abstraction to general principles or ideals. In so doing, it can verge on an ahistorical idealism or intellectual reductionism that wrenches biblical statements out of their social, historical and covenantal context and converts them into timeless ethical norms. This is particularly apparent in attempts to isolate timeless, supracultural principles in scriptural teaching.[55] But did the biblical authors intend their specific statements to be abstracted into abiding, universal principles? One further temptation of this method is to blunt the radical edge of specific commands in Scripture, such as those of the Sermon on the Mount, by transposing them into bland principles or ideal dispositions.[56] Clearly there are 'ideals' in Scripture, but they are not timeless metaphysical values but visions of a concrete state of affairs in the future toward which the historical community is beckoned (e.g. Isa 11:6f). In short, a concern for divining prescriptive principles and ideals can divorce biblical ethics from the exigencies of specific contexts and persons.[57]

(b) The procedure of deriving principles becomes a very *subjective exercise*, too easily reflecting the bias of the interpreter.[58] Different interpreters may derive different principles from the same text. What criteria exist for deciding who is right? Rules of thumb can be suggested for isolating key principles (e.g. differentiating between what the Bible records and what it commends; seeking the intention or goal of a particular instruction; ensuring consistency with overarching themes, etc.), but such guidelines can still yield diverse results. The distinction between 'rules' and 'principles' is also rather fluid. Is 'thou shalt not kill' an underlying principle of the value of human life, or a specific rule forbidding murder within the context of the covenantal community?

(c) As an ethical method, it is too *vague and atomistic.* Sometimes the principles deduced are so general or banal as to be virtually useless in granting specific direction in contemporary reflection.[59] Moreover, there is more to ethical life than applying a series of isolated principles. Especially in social ethics, some overall model or social theory is needed to show how the principles interrelate and promote a particular way of life.[60] What happens, for example, when two principles conflict (e.g. the principle of private property ownership and the principle of economic justice, or the principles of justice and mercy)? How are the principles to be related to each other in an overall framework?

(d) The *mode of application* of biblical principles or ideals in different circumstances is more complex than often assumed. Where present reality does not wholly conform to the ideal or principle, some compromises or approximations are necessary. How do we decide how much compromise is required or justified, if indeed compromises, even unavoidable compromises, can strictly be 'justified'?[61] Furthermore, a principle derived from a biblical command or text related to a specific socio-political context should ideally be reapplied in a contemporary context that is analogous to the biblical context. How are these analogies to be identified?

Now such cautions as these do not render the prescriptive appeal to the Bible wholly illegitimate. By no means. Moral rules *do* have an indispensable role in ethical life, and it *is* possible to identify important concerns or principles within biblical morality. According to James Childress, biblical authority is distorted if the rules and principles contained in Scripture are ignored or down-played.[62] But equally the nature and function of Scripture are also distorted if the Bible is reduced to a collection of ahistorical moral prescriptions, and Christian moral experience is impoverished if it is equated with the mechanical application of a norm-based system of rules.

The Illuminative Use of Scripture

In this approach the Bible is viewed not as a source book of moral norms or prescriptions but as a resource for basic values and perspectives that can inform contemporary decision-making. It sets forth a moral and theological framework, or symbolic universe, that provides the context for considering ethical decisions. Recent scholarship has tended to reject the prescriptive in favour of an illuminative use of Scripture, for both theological and practical reasons. Theologically, there is, especially in Protestant scholarship, a dread of legalism, a fear of substituting genuine obedience to the sovereign Word of God with a rationally-devised system of ethics, which might then become a ground for commending ourselves to God.[63] Practically, the plurality of literary forms in the Bible, the cultural distance that separates the 'then' of the biblical text from the 'now' of today, and the sheer complexity of the moral questions we face today, mean that biblical prescriptions are inadequate to the task of moral guidance. But ethical decisions can still be *illuminated* by, and must be consonant with, the central concerns and commitments of the Bible. Scripture thus provides a kind of 'revealed reality' that determines the basic direction and orientation of Christian morality.

The illuminative or perspectival use of Scripture can take many forms. To illustrate, we shall consider two methodological procedures that seek to allow Scripture to elucidate contemporary moral situations.

1. Reasoning from Biblical Images

Earlier we noted how Scripture provides both a compelling portrait of the human condition and an account of a God who *acts and speaks* in particular historical events. If history is the arena of divine revelation, then Christian ethical decision-making needs to be based on a 'reading of the times', on a decision about what God is saying or doing in contemporary events. To determine this, Scripture should be consulted. The answer will come not from the prescriptive commandments or moral norms of Scripture but by a process of discernment guided by the central images of the text. Since God is not capricious, the patterns central to biblical revelation and theological generalisations about the character of God can be used to detect the continuing manifestation of God in current affairs. Just as the exilic prophets used the exodus to interpret release from Babylonian captivity, so modern Christians can use the images and symbols of Scripture, and supremely the way of the Cross, to uncover God's actions in the present, and hence decide an appropriate ethical response.

The strength of this approach is its movement away from isolated proof-texts and principles toward a wholistic application of biblical revelation. The concern to root ethics in a theologically-sound image of God, and God's definitive manifestation in the Crucified One, is also important. This makes Christian morality distinctive, not merely as a result of accumulated moral judgements about particular matters, but because of the theological world-view that gives meaning, direction and content to ethical conduct.

But there are also problems with this approach.

(a) The key problem in an appeal to the guiding images of Scripture is *knowing the right ones to select.* 'Some current writers', observes Spohn, 'seem to have abandoned proof-texting for 'proof-theming' – selecting biblical images that support moral conclusions they have reached on other grounds'.[64] History has witnessed many times the tragic results of Christians choosing the conquest of Canaan or Samson's destruction of the Philistines as the central paradigm for discerning God's present will. Some criteria (or 'rules'?) are needed to avoid such distortions.[65]

(b) Even if such negative images are excluded, there remains a *wide diversity of positive images* that might be used to grant perspective on contemporary events, each potentially yielding a different conclusion. It is too easy to make a moral judgement on the basis of personal or political values, and then find some biblical image to support it from the variety available. Indeed, the *same* image can produce diverse judgements; the exodus has been used, for example, to justify both violent liberation movements and to commend non-violent resistance to oppressive regimes.[66] In short, whether we allow a single privileged image or set of images to guide discernment, or if we seek to do justice to the variety of images in Scripture, the result may well be ambiguous.

(c) While biblical images and themes provide an important framework for approaching specific decisions, surely Scripture can also offer a little more *normative clarity* on specific concerns. The exclusion of any normative authority for Scriptural commands, laws or principles threatens to undermine the distinctively Christian character of Christian ethics, and allow too much place for subjective judgement. While the Bible's ethical function should not be reduced to that of a prescriptive code, there *are* matters about which the Bible speaks to us in the form of direct moral address, and does so repeatedly and consistently. This suggests that there are certain moral imperatives, such as care for the poor and oppressed, that are not optional for those who claim allegiance to the God of the Bible.

2. *Reasoning by Analogy*

The second methodological procedure seeks to establish a connection between the current situation and appropriate biblical teaching by a process of analogical and dialectical reasoning. Biblical texts may be accepted as relevant for today if there is a significant similarity between the situation addressed in Scripture and the situation that pertains now. Conversely, contemporary actions may be evaluated by a comparison to similar actions under similar circumstances recorded in the Bible. In this way, the Bible becomes a collection of models or paradigms that can be mobilised when a significant parallel exists between circumstances then and now.

The principle of analogy can operate in a prescriptive fashion, with the pattern of the biblical model having binding authority in comparable circumstances today. The illuminative use of analogy is somewhat looser. Its aim is to *learn* from biblical examples, not necessarily to duplicate them in particulars. The function of biblical paradigms is neither to provide an external goal toward which we work, nor a timeless ideal which we strive to apply, nor a legal rule which we obey. Instead it serves to *inform and influence* present actions. The present community is free to make the paradigm its own, to adapt it into the texture and fabric of its own historically-conditioned setting.[67] Schüssler-Fiorenza captures this distinction by suggesting that Scripture provides not fixed *archetypes* that later Christians must conform to in particulars, but open-ended *prototypes,* dynamic models of structural transformation that are exemplary but may be reshaped under current circumstances. Scriptural prototypes are initial models that can be reformed, refined, even improved on, although future designs should retain some recognisable resemblance to the original.[68]

Three points can be made in favour of such analogical reasoning. The first is that it presupposes a *dialogical* rather than a unidirectional relationship between text and interpreter. Instead of first attempting to discern from a neutral standpoint, what the text 'meant' in the past, then asking about its contemporary relevance, past and present are brought into dialectical relationship. The past illuminates the present, while the needs of the present raise new questions and cast new light on the past. Instead of being paralysed, as some interpreters are, by the historical and cultural discontinuities between then and now, analogical reasoning presumes there are legitimate connections between the patterns of human action in the biblical world and today.[69] Second, the biblical writers themselves often discern analogical or typological relationships between past and present events, using the 'type' to grant insight or revelation into the later 'anti-type'.[70] The New Testament writers do not engage in historical exegesis for its own sake, but make illuminating connections between events recorded in the canon and their own present situation. Third, such an approach honours the dynamic and historical character of biblical revelation. Rather than providing a fixed deposit of static, ahistorical truths, the Bible points beyond itself to a God who remains active in human history and who calls for faithful responses from his people in contemporary situations not envisaged in Scripture, but nonetheless analogous to previous situations faced by the people of God in biblical times.

At the same time, the use of analogy encounters several difficulties.

(a) Some critics would suggest that the value of seeking analogies is vitiated by the fact that every ethical situation is *sui generis.* 'The hard fact of the matter is', says Robin Scroggs, 'that historical situations in which ethical/ theological judgements emerge are unique. Unique situations cannot be superimposed on one another. Thus the principle of analogy must seriously be called into question'.[71] There is some truth in this. Decision-making situations *are* unique; actions followed in one setting cannot be replicated in another. But what is learned in one unique situation can be adapted and *re*-applied (not duplicated) in another. The principle of analogy requires a significant *correspondence* between situations in the text and today, not an absolute *identity.*

(b) But there is still difficulty in determining the *scope of the correspondence*. Biblical texts derive their meaning from the total cultural-linguistic system to which they belong. In using a biblical example for analogical elucidation, to what extent should there be a correspondence between the wider environment of the text and that of today? (If a comprehensive analogy were drawn between the New Testament world and modern society, biblical scholars and professional ethicists would correspond to the scribes and Pharisees, whom Jesus condemned as bereft of genuine ethical insight!).[72]

(c) This highlights the *complexity* of determining what is entailed in following biblical paradigms in our modern setting. The modern world is so different from the world of the biblical text that contemporary equivalents to biblical paradigms may require strategies so different that there will be little resemblance to the alleged paradigm. Jesus enjoins his followers to do good and lend without interest, to share what little they had with those in need. A modern analogy would probably require a complex and sophisticated socioeconomic response to the needy, within the framework of an international trading economy where buying bananas at the local supermarket has an impact on the poor in the Third World.[73] It is arguably at this point that the *Social Justice Statement* is most vulnerable. Is it enough to point to biblical paradigms which embody concern for the poor without discussing the possible shape of contemporary analogies?

(d) The most significant problem lies in the area of the 'control' of analogy, that is, of determining how a legitimate connection is made between biblical text and contemporary circumstance.[74] If present events are in control, there is the danger of selecting biblical analogies that merely confirm prior ethical commitments or personal interest on the part of the decision-maker. If one believes, for example, that liberation from oppression is the chief need of the present situation, one might select events such as the exodus or Jesus' inaugural address in Luke for the purposes of analogical elucidation. The danger here is one of exploiting the Bible as simply a rhetorical support for strategies that have actually been derived from secular sources. If, on the other hand, one starts with biblical models then seeks contemporary applications, there is the danger of imposing biblical models arbitrarily on current situations on the basis of rather superficial resemblances. What constitutes sufficient evidence that the circumstances in our time are similar enough to those of biblical times to justify application of the biblical model?

Again these concerns are real. But the problem of control, of avoiding a merely decorative use of the Bible to embellish pre-established moral judgements, is common to all interpretive strategies. In reality one never 'starts' with either the biblical text or the contemporary situation; both are always present, and there is a constant dialectic between them. This mutual interrogation of readers by the text, and the text in light of the readers' present situation, permits a progressive refinement in faithful appropriation of the text. The only ultimate control are the checks and balances offered by the wider community of God's people honestly seeking to live faithfully before God in light of Scripture. This leads directly to our third way of appreciating the moral import of the Bible.

The Formative Use of Scripture

Common to both prescriptive and the illuminative handlings of Scripture is the assumption that ethical decision-making is predominantly an individual affair guided by rational and theological analysis. The key questions are methodological: which interpretive strategies are most effective for apprehending the moral role of Scripture? And the test of validity is the universalisability of the method for all contexts and situations.

Little has been said so far about two matters that fundamentally influence both ethical decision-making and biblical interpretation, whatever the method employed. They are the *personal character* of the moral agent, and the location of decision-makers within a wider *community of discourse.* When these considerations are addressed, a third way of thinking about the moral use of Scripture comes into view, namely its *formative role* in shaping character and building a Christian community. Recently, there has been a definite shift of interest among biblical scholars and ethicists from 'trying to assimilate biblical morality to the model of deductive argumentation to an interest in Scripture as foundational to the formation of communities of moral agency'.[75]

In the formative approach the relevance of the Bible for ethics goes beyond providing appropriate verses, principles, images or analogies for resolving specific ethical dilemmas. It also lies in its role of transforming the character, vision, values, motivations and intentions of moral agents, both individually and collectively. Scripture affects the decision-maker as well as informs the decisions to be made. Of course, the importance of personal moral virtues has long been stressed in Christian ethics, but increasing attention is now being given to the inter-connection between character formation, community building and Scripture reading. In their recent excellent book on the topic, Fowl and Jones insist that,

> ... because there is no way to talk about moral decisions apart from people's contexts, convictions, and commitments, a preoccupation with decisions made by isolated individuals distorts our conception of ethics in general and the relation of Scripture to Christian ethics in

> particular. An adequate conception of ethics requires attention to issues of character and formation of character in and through socially-embodied traditions.[76]

In what follows we will comment on these aspects sequentially, although it is their interrelationship that is most significant.

1. Scripture and Character-Formation

One of the clear presumptions of New Testament ethics is that personal conversion and transformation in self-understanding lies at the root of ethical behaviour.[77] For Paul, the work of grace serves to *liberate* us from our bondage to 'the works of the flesh', to impart new *motivation* for ethical obedience energised by gratitude for God's undeserved love and mercy, to give new *content* to ethical life (patterned on the self-giving love of Christ), to enable moral *discernment* no longer dependent on the 'letter' of the law, and to *empower* a new level of ethical attainment which spontaneously produces 'the fruit of the Spirit' and thus 'fulfils' (not simply obeys)[78] the just requirements of the law.' Moral conversion and ongoing character-formation are considered crucial by Paul to engender a true obedience. Indicative and imperative are inseparable; believers are called 'to be' what they have already 'become' in Christ. Accordingly, 'the starting point of an authentically Christian ethics is the recognition that the conversion of the individual leads to a new obedience, a new lifestyle, a new ethic'.[79]

Scripture stands in a two-fold relation to this process. On the one hand the disciplined reading of the biblical account promotes and nurtures character-transformation.[80] And it is the biblical account in its entirety, not just its explicitly ethical content, that nourishes character development. It names and helps to form virtues and values, it identifies and encourages obligations and it fosters and renews moral vision. It engenders a new orientation toward God, the world and others; it affects what sort of persons we are; it functions to 'renew our minds' so that we may 'discern what is the will of God' (Rom 12:2); it evokes attitudes and affections of the heart by disclosing to us what God is like and what God has accomplished for us. In other words, the Scriptures have the capacity when illumined by the Spirit to touch 'the concrete regions of the heart' from whence true moral conduct emerges.[81] As we are shaped and reshaped by the concerns of Scripture, we are equipped to think and act in relation to ethical questions in a way consistent with the biblical account of God's will.[82]

On the other hand, as the lifelong process of character-formation and transformation continues, believers are increasingly enabled to interpret Scripture wisely. The goal of biblical interpretation is not just correct understanding, but the faithful *embodiment* of Scripture in life. Christians are required to 'present their bodies' in obedience, not just their minds, if they are to discern God's will and be transformed in character (Rom 12.1). This is one of the most consistent and recurring themes of biblical teaching. Well-formed character does not guarantee proper discernment, but the discernment of God's will in Scripture cannot be evaluated apart from the virtues of the Christ-like character it produces in the interpreter.

2. *Scripture and Community-Formation*

The formation of individual character always occurs in and through participation in communities. Individuals do not exist prior to, or apart from, community but always in relation to community. We are taught to make moral judgements and to exercise approved qualities in the context of particular historical communities. We learn to be virtuous by observing and copying others in the community; their example inspires us to be virtuous. Ethics, then, is not just the history of abstract ideas but the history of communities.[83] This insight has significant implications for appreciating the moral role of Scripture, not least because Scripture itself is the product of, and charter document for, a faith community with its own particular history.

It means, in the first place, that the fundamental 'analogy' between the biblical text and the current context lies not in some ethical situation or event but in the believing community itself. The distinctive social reality of the Christian community is the primary form of continuity with the biblical world. And it is within this community that the Scriptures assume their authority; 'the church is the community defined by its allegiance to the Scriptures or as shaped by scriptural witness'.[84]

From this it follows, second, that the ethical discernment of Scripture is a *communal task*. Scripture was originally addressed, not to individuals but to specific communities called into being by God to embody a particular way of life.[85] The texts fulfilled a *social function* in promoting a lifestyle of non-conformity to the world. Similar, in some respects counter-cultural, communities are therefore the most appropriate context for their interpretation today. Discernment of the moral import of Scripture is not just the job of specialists; it is a communal responsibility involving every member of the congregation (1 Cor 14:26, 29). The role of specialists is to contribute to the communal process. Yoder discusses, for instance, the distinctive contributions to be made by 'agents of direction' (prophets, 1 Cor 14:3, 29), 'agents of memory' (scribes, or scholars, Matt 13:52), 'agents of linguistic self-consciousness' (teachers, Jas 3:18; 2 Tim 1: 13; 2:16), and 'agents of order and due process' (overseers/bishops/elders, Ac 15:13, 28).[86]

Third, the goal of interpretation must be the faithful *embodiment* or re-socialisation of the moral vision of Scripture, viz., the formation of a common life that reflects the values, convictions and practices related in the text. This is what the 'authority' of Scripture means – the capacity of Scripture to form a people who live in a way that continues the story of God in the world.[87] The normative authority of the text lies in the concrete social strategies it uses to engender such a radical community. Consequently, in Meeks' words, 'a hermeneutical strategy entails a social strategy', and at both ends of the interpretive task. At one end the social function of the text for the biblical community must be uncovered. Sociological and historical tools can be used to discover the impact the earliest Christian communities had in their socio-political contexts. At the other end the text can be used to suggest comparable social configurations today; and 'the hermeneutical circle is not completed until the text finds a fitting social embodiment'.[88] The modern community ought to be analogous to the first Christian communities by its conformity to the paradigmatic social challenges they presented in their own socio-political contexts. The moral authority of Scripture thus lies in the social identities and social relationships it calls forth in the believing community. Accordingly, 'moral norms are justified not as transcriptions of biblical rules, or even as references to key narrative themes, but as coherent social embodiments of a community formed by Scripture'.[89]

Fourth, the commitment to embody the witness of Scripture in a common life is essential in order to *adjudicate interpretive disputes.* Moral ratification is not principally a matter of deductive reasoning or individualistic intuitivism, although rules, principles, analogies and individual judgement may all play a role; it is the outcome of a communal process of discernment in congregations committed to the 'hermeneutics of obedience'.[90] The interpretive options chosen can only be confirmed in the praxis or lived-discipleship of the community.

> The aim of Scriptural interpretation is to shape our common life in the situations in which we find ourselves according to the characters, convictions and practices related in Scripture. Because no one interpretive strategy can deliver *the* meaning of a text, there is no hard

> and fast method that will ensure faithful interpretation. No particular community of believers can be sure of what a faithful interpretation of Scripture will entail in any specific situation until it actually engages in the hard process of conversation, argument, discussion, prayer and practice.[91]

Finally, interpreters who stress the formative role of Scripture often (but not always) give maximum value to the *narrative quality* of Scripture for ethics. Not only is 'story' the dominant genre in the Bible, but the completed canon tells one narrationally-unified story (or meta-story) that starts with 'in the beginning' and closes with 'come Lord Jesus'. Current scholarship sees great significance in both these facts. The story-mode of Scripture is believed to be crucial to its moral authority because stories signify characteristic ways of thinking and acting that shape the self-understanding of their hearers. All good stories have the effect of drawing the audience into the action, engaging our emotions, encouraging identification with the narrative figures, so that we experience what the characters experience in the story.[92] In this way stories create a basic orientation to the world; they foster convictions and commitments, sharpen sensitivities and inspire virtues and values. Stories are self-involving and self-revealing in a way that moral philosophy, rules and principles are not. Stories are also fundamental to communal solidarity and identity. 'We are story-telling creatures', Birch and Rasmussen observe, 'compelled to make sense of our experience through recollection and narrative. Narration … gives form and meaning to our experience'.[93] Shared stories express the common origins, history, memories and values of a people, while religious stories relate such experience to matters of ultimate significance. Accordingly, the story of Scripture, and in particular the stories of Jesus, have a character- and community-constituting power. The story imparts a distinctive way of life which inculcates certain character-virtues and moral dispositions in its recipients.

There is, then, a growing conviction that the contribution of the Bible to ethics lies at the level of character- and community-formation, not primarily at the level of rules or principles. Scripture serves as a reminder of the kind of people we are to become and the kind of way we are to be present in the world.[94] Its moral authority lies in the socially revolutionary strategies it commends for handling wealth, power, violence and social prejudice.[95] The connection between what the text 'meant' and what it 'means' today is the concrete community which seeks analogous expressions of social life. Praxis is the criterion of verification of ethical claims and injunctions. As Hays explains:

> ... knowledge of God's will *follows* the community's submission and transformation. Why? because until we see the text lived, we cannot begin to conceive what it means. Until we see God's power at work among us we do not know what we are reading. Thus the most crucial hermeneutical task is the formation of communities seeking to live under the word.[96]

With the demise of Constantinian Christendom, this emphasis on the social embodiment of Scripture's moral witness in distinctive communities of faith and witness is of strategic importance. It is not an entirely new emphasis; the 'believers church' tradition of the radical Reformation, where voluntary communities of dissent embodied an alternative to both the authoritarianism of the Catholic *Magisterium* on the one hand, and the arbitrary individualism of later Protestantism on the other, has something important to offer the contemporary church. The work of John Howard Yoder is becoming very influential in this respect.[97] The model of the 'Scripture-shaped community' of discernment does not 'solve' the issue of how we use Scripture for specific ethical direction, but it does put the question in a different light. The primary question is not 'what should I do', but 'what distinctive *form of life* does Scripture call us to?'

At the same time this emphasis on the formative role of Scripture involves its own range of quandaries.

(a) Some critics level a charge of 'fideism' or 'sectarianism' against it. They detect an elaboration of ethics from a self-enclosed religious standpoint that is not accessible or accountable to the broader secular community. They also fear the loss of an intelligible Christian contribution to the public discourse of the wider community. However, in response it must be said that there is an inescapable tension in Christian ethics between commonality and distinctiveness, between universality and particularity, a tension that is present in the New Testament itself. There is something unavoidably alien about the values derived from the way of Christ that cannot be universalised or validated by the wider community of discourse.[98] On the other hand, insofar as Christians live simultaneously in both Christian and non-Christian communities, and are fully involved in both, they will remain open to cultural challenge, receptive to the wisdom and perspectives of outsiders and ready to contribute Christian perspectives to communal discourse and social ethics.[99] Indeed, a willingness to be interrogated by the world, to be open to outsiders and to be committed to the wellbeing and transformation of the wider world are essential ingredients of healthy Christian communities.[100] Such features were characteristic of New Testament communities.[101]

(b) The use of communities and their praxis as the basic analogy with the biblical texts raises the question of what is meant by 'Christian community'. The term may be used today to refer to realities very different from the tightly-knit and disciplined local churches of the first-century. It includes the larger institutional church, with elaborate power structures and longstanding traditions. The notion of analogous social strategies works best if the *form* as well as the commitments of the contemporary community are analogous to those of the 'household' churches on the New Testament, viz., intimate in fellowship, inclusive in social make-up, egalitarian in relationships and charismatic in operation. But, as Fowl and Jones lament, there is a distressing paucity of vital Christian communities in the contemporary Western world; and such common life as we do experience is often impoverished.[102] In some respects, the 'base' Christian communities of Latin America, Africa and Asia offer much closer analogies to those of New Testament times.

(c) Aside from the need to rehabilitate authentic Christian community in the West, 'a huge remaining question for ethicists is how to guarantee the truth of the interpretations *by* the community'.[103] Corrupt character and self-serving falsehood can become as embedded in the fabric of a community's life as readily as in an individual's, as demonstrated by the German Church of the Nazi era and the Dutch Reformed Church of South Africa during the days of apartheid. How is communal deception to be prevented or exposed? What should guide individuals in standing against disobedient or misinformed communities? If social embodiment is the *sine qua non* of ethical verification, how does one evaluate communal experience? Are there are any broader norms of community and praxis to which local communities remain accountable? How do communities know whether certain features of New Testament practice, such as non-violence or economic redistribution, are to be reproduced in their own situation in order to remain faithful? Are not certain criteria that transcend a community's partial perspective on truth necessary? Are not rationally-defensible methods of moral analysis open to cross-communal testing and validation still essential?

(d) Several queries also attach to the central place some give to 'story' or narrative in the educative role of Scripture. Story is only one element in the communicating structure of culture, along with customs, rituals, laws, sacred symbols, and the like, and is only one among several genres in the canon. Why then should narrative be made the governing pattern of moral formation and normative ethics?[104] There is also no need for story to be set in tension with moral rules and principles. As long as the moral imperatives of Scripture are allowed to function initially within the story-world of the text and not be abstracted into universal rules, they have an indispensable role in facilitating the contemporary embodiment of the text. There is, in fact, danger of a different kind of abstraction in the narrative method, with the historical particularity of Abraham, Moses and Jesus being reduced to specimens of a new kind of universal, namely 'narrative forms'.[105] Then there are the questions of how we avoid reading the story in a highly selective fashion. Is it possible for people in positions of privilege and power to 'hear' stories oriented toward the poor and judgemental toward the rich? The social location of the modern faith community decisively influences, and can easily determine, how the text is understood.

Conclusion

The preceding discussion demonstrates that while there is general agreement that the Bible is to be used as an authority in Christian ethics, there is disagreement about *how* the Bible's witness is best actualised. Traditionally, most attention has centred on the need for a universal, rationally-defensible hermeneutical method that individual believers may employ in any situation. Individualism (what individuals, divested of their local traditions and parochial attachments, have in common as rational human beings) and universalism (what is categorically applicable to all situations) have been the guiding beacons of moral philosophy since the Enlightenment.[106] Recent discussion however has shifted the focus from 'proper' methodology to the role of the church as a hermeneutical community committed to the social embodiment of the text it reveres. This 'formative' emphasis reminds us that personal character and communal process are absolutely indispensable to a faithful handling of the text.

With respect to the *Social Justice Statement*, this implies that before, and as well as, calling on the state to seek social justice, New Zealand churches themselves must be practicing what they preach. Whether the ten denominations involved, and their individual congregations, may be justly regarded as eschatological colonies of peace and justice is a moot point. But insofar as the church leaders seek to use Scripture to educate and sensitise their members to the need for social justice in the wider community, a commitment to become such counter-cultural communities is crucial. It is noteworthy, therefore, that neither the *Social Justice Statement* nor the associated study book has significant comment on this dimension, although the passing reference to the 'way of life' of church members in §.5 and the existence of church foodbanks, night shelters and social service programmes (also mentioned in the *Statement* in §§.16, 43) demonstrate that such a concern is certainly not absent. And the *Statement* itself is the outcome of a communal process, at least among the specialists.

I am not suggesting that Christians have no right to offer social and political critique until they have put their own house in order; that is a recipe for political quietism that would compromise the church's responsibility in society. Nor am I proposing that the churches meekly accept that it is their responsibility rather than the state's to meet the needs of the socially disadvantaged, and so cease criticising the government for failing to do so; that the church is God's primary agent of redeeming love and justice does not mean that the state is exempt from its own responsibilities in these areas. What I am saying is that unless Christian congregations are as vigorously committed to embodying in their own common life the values they commend to the government, they are devaluing the primary moral function of Scripture, its role in creating alternative communities of Christ-like character.

As such communities seek to apply Scripture to their historical situation, the full storehouse of the biblical witness should be appropriated. This will require attention to themes and analogies ('illuminative use') as well as rules and principles ('prescriptive use') of relevance. Methodological dichotomies that set one approach against another should be avoided; 'the task of the teacher will rather be to contribute to the community's awareness that every decision includes elements of principle, elements of character and of due process, and elements of utility'.[107] A methodological pluralism is demanded, not only by the inherent limitations of each method in isolation, as explored above, but by the evidence of Scripture itself. The New Testament writers appeal to written Scripture in several different modes. Scripture is treated as a source of *moral rules or laws,* as in New Testament appeals to the Decalogue[108] (e.g. Matt 5:21-48; Mk 10:17-22; Rom 7:7; Eph 6:2; Jas 2:11); as a source of *ideals or principles*, as in Jesus' appeal to creation norms[109] (e.g. Mk 10:6), or his linking of Deut 6:4-5 with Leviticus 19:18 to form the double love command (Mk 12:28-31 par); as a source of *analogies or precedents for action*, as undergirds the entire argument of Hebrews and biblical typology in general; as a collection of *narratives* that characterise appropriate actions and self-understanding, such as in Jesus' appeal to the stories of Noah and Lot (Lk 17:26-37); as a source of *images and themes* that help pinpoint God's action in present history, as in Stephen's apology (Ac 7:2-53) or Paul's sermon in Pisidian Antioch (Ac 14:14-43); and as supplying a *symbolic universe* that illuminates both the human condition and the character of God, as in the diagnosis of the fallen human condition in Rom 1:18-32, or the characterisation of God in Matt 5:43-48.

This multiplicity of ways in which the Scriptural text is appropriated suggests that all of them are potentially legitimate modes for reflection on the normative role of Scripture today, and that no one mode (such as law or narrative or principle) should be allowed to overrule all others.[110] The need for methodological discipline does not imply methodological uniformity. The key issue is deciding which method of appropriation is most suitable to particular texts. Initially effort should be made to correlate the mode of interpretation with the mode of moral discourse employed by the text itself, so that narratives are not read as rules, or analogies turned into laws or timeless principles. Of course, treating laws as laws and principles as principles still leaves open the question of how they apply today.

How then is Scripture used within the *Social Justice Statement* itself? The *Statement* is not, of course, a thoroughgoing exercise in biblical exegesis, nor should it be. There is a general appeal to 'the values taught in the Scriptures' (§.1) and to fundamental 'principles ... in the teaching of Jesus Christ and the Hebrew Scriptures' (§.6), especially the primacy of love (§.13,19); but apart from love it does not anchor these principles in specific texts. The same applies to its more general appeal of the character of 'a God who is merciful' (§.4). The few texts it mentions are employed in a rather loose, illuminative fashion. Those used to introduce the major sections of the document serve an illustrative or literary function; the wording of the text is used to epitomise the socio-political assertions that follow, even though in their original context the texts have a quite different focus. So Paul's statement that spiritual manifestations are for the good of the whole Christian community (1 Cor 12:7) is used to introduce the political concept of 'the common good'; his comment on the diversity of charismata (Rom 12:6) is used to illustrate the evils of unemployment; Jesus' warning that judgement faces disciples who do not attend to the needs of the 'least of their brothers and sisters' (Matt 25:40) is used to encourage a social policy that cares for the poor in general.

Such interpretation of these texts could not justified by the normal canons of historical exegesis; they are used in an evocative, even decorative, fashion. A less charitable interpretation could dismiss this as proof-texting or even a simplistic biblicism. But examination of the study book *Making Choices* reveals a more extensive and nuanced engagement with Scripture. Again the emphasis is on biblical 'values', 'principles', and 'themes' illuminating Christian perspectives on society rather than on elaborating a coherent, biblically-informed social or political ethic, or on exploring the social character of the Christian community itself. The former is a complex task falling outside the scope of the book, but perhaps the latter deserves more attention than it receives. For the supreme calling of the Christian community is not merely to be a critic of trends in secular society but to embody a distinctive pattern of life, foreshadowed in Scripture, that challenges society with an alternative vision of life under God's reign and that enables Christians to become ever wiser in their reading of the biblical text.

Notes

1. Micah 6:8; Jn 10:10; 13; 34;1 Cor12:7, 13:3; Rom12:6; Matt 25:40.
2. Cf. J.H. Yoder, *The Christian Witness to the State,* Newton, KA. Faith and Life Press, 1964, pp. 60-73.
3. R. Smithies and H. Wilson (eds), *Making Choices: Social Justice For Our Times,* Wellington: GP Print, 1993, p. 12.
4. Cf. Bruce C. Birch and Larry L. Rasmussen, *Bible and Ethics in the Christian Life,* Minneapolis: Augsburg, 1989 rev. ed., p. 38ff.
5. Cf. Alister E. McGrath, 'Doctrine and Ethics', *Journal of the Evangelical Theological Society,* 34/2, 1991, pp. 145-56; Jochem Douma, 'The Use of Scripture in Ethics', *European Journal of Theology,* 1/2, 1992, p. 113f.
6. Certain demands are made of Christians in the New Testament that go beyond natural human prudence or philosophically justifiable morality – preference for the outcast, costly service even unto death, helping others with no expectation of recompense, loving one's enemies, taking others more seriously than oneself. Christian ethics does not just require us to love our neighbour, but to love in the way specifically modelled by Jesus in the Gospels. On the love commands, see the stimulating discussion by Paul Ricouer, 'The Golden Rule: Exegetical and Theological Perplexities', *New Testament Studies,* 36, 1990, pp. 392-97.
7. Cf. Micah 6:3-5,8; Exodus 20:1-17.
8. The precise meaning of the *imitatio Christi* motif in the New Testament is debated, but it seems clear that the early Christians believed that by imitating Jesus, they were learning to imitate God (note, for example, the use of 'perfect' in Matt 5:48 and 19:21). For a survey of later uses of the motif, see Margaret R. Miles, 'Imitation of Christ: Is It Possible in the Twentieth Century?', *Princeton Seminary Bulletin,* 10/1, 1989, pp. 7-22.

9. It is noteworthy that the first Christians were not specially concerned to maintain an 'ethical distance' between themselves and their non-Christian environment, except in areas where contemporary values clashed with those of the gospel. Recent studies have shown that in their paraenesis, New Testament authors draw upon well-established *topoi,* and in so doing align themselves with ethically enlightened members of wider Jewish and Greco-Roman society. This is not to deny a genuine distinctiveness about certain Christian values, nor to weaken the oft-repeated call to Christian non-conformity in the New Testament (e.g. Rom 12:1-2). It is to rather to discern two complementary themes in early Christian ethical teaching, one that recognises the common humanity of Christian and non-Christian in virtue of creation, the other that stresses the eschatological distinctiveness of Christian lifestyle.
10. See Lisa Sowle Cahill, *Between the Sexes: Foundations for a Christian Ethics of Sexuality,* Philadelphia: Fortress Press, 1985, pp. 5-6, 145-48.
11. See, for example, Gal 5: 16-26; 6:1; Rom 8:13, 28; 9:1; 14:17; 15:13, 30; 2 Cor 3:18; 6:6; Col 1:8.
12. See, for example, Jn 14:25-31; 15:21-16:15; Ac 15:28; Rom 8:4-6, 14; Gal 5:16, 18, 25; cf. Rom 8:13; Gal 6:8; 1 Cor 2:12.
13. 1 Cor 3:16; 6:19; 12:13; 14:29, 38; 1 Thess 5:19-22; 2 Thess 2:2; 1 Jn 4:1.
14. W.D. Davies, 'Paul and the Law: Pitfalls in Interpretation' in M.D. Hooker and S.G. Wilson (eds), *Paul and Paulinism,* London: SPCK, 1982, p. 11.
15. Cf. John F. Kilner, 'A Pauline Approach to Ethical Decision-Making', *Interpretation,* 43/4, 1989, pp. 366-79.
16. James M. Gustafson, 'The Place of Scripture in Christian Ethics: A Methodological Study', *Interpretation,* 24/4, 1970, p. 455. Gustafson affirms that the role of Scripture is to inform Christian moral judgements, 'but it does not by itself determine what they ought to be. That determination is done by persons and communities as finite moral agents responsible to God' (p. 455). So too Edward LeRoy Long, Jr., 'The Use of the Bible in Christian Ethics', *Interpretation,* 19/2, 1965, p. 451; Allen Verhey, 'Bible in Christian Ethics' in J. Macquarrie and J. Childress, *A New Dictionary of Christian Ethics,* London: SCM, 1986, p. 57, 60f.
17. According to Barnabas Lindars, although the Reformers claimed to transfer authority in ethical matters from the pronouncements of the *Magisterium* of the church to the Bible, their moral traditions 'were largely prefabricated, and really only employed the Bible as the authoritative sanction for them', 'Bible and Christian Ethics', *Theology* 76/634, 1973, p. 181. Yoder similarly urges that 'Protestant scholasticism ... claimed that the Bible was the only moral authority and announced a fundamental suspicion of moral discernment ... [which] claims rootage in reason, nature, and tradition. Yet when this official Protestantism turned to the problems of administering its own society, there resulted at the time no profound difference between it and Catholicism on any practical moral issues: divorce, usury, war, or truth-telling', J.H. Yoder, 'The Hermeneutics of Peoplehood: A Protestant Perspective on Practical Moral Reasoning', *Journal of Religious Ethics,* 10, 1982, p. 45. See also *idem,* John H. Yoder, *'Authority of the Canon'* in W. M. Swartley (ed.), *Essays on Biblical Interpretation,* Elkhart, IN: IMS, 1984, pp. 265-272.
18. More ink has been spilled asserting *that* the Bible possesses authority than in reflecting on what is meant by 'authority' itself. For helpful discussions on this, see N.T. Wright,

'How Can the Bible be Authoritative?', *Vox Evangelica,* 21, 1991, pp. 7-32; Stanley Hauerwas, 'The Moral Authority of Scripture: the Politics and Ethics of Remembering', *Interpretation,* 34, 1980, pp. 356-70.

19. The particular model used to interpret New Testament eschatology has been the most decisive consideration in determining how scholars have judged the contemporary relevance of New Testament ethics. See the survey in Robin Scroggs, 'The New Testament and Ethics: How Do We Get From There to Here?', *Perspectives in Religious Studies,* 11/4, 1984, pp. 77-93 (esp. pp. 84-89).
20. For brief surveys of those with such views, see I.H. Marshall, 'Using the Bible in Ethics' in David F. Wright (ed.), *Essays in Evangelical Social Ethics,* Exeter: Paternoster Press, 1979, pp. 45-49; W.M. Swartley, *Slavery, Sabbath, War and Women,* Scottdale: Herald Press, 1983, pp. 204-11; David Cook, *The Moral Maze,* London: SPCK, 1983, pp. 46-50; V. P. Furnish, *The Moral Teaching of Paul,* Nashville: Abingdon, 1985, pp. 18-23.
21. I.H. Marshall, 'Using the Bible', p. 39f.
22. Gustafson, 'Place of Scripture', p. 448f.
23. Ibid., p. 449.
24. In Paul's paraenesis, written Scripture serves primarily to confirm, reinforce or illuminate ethical demands that are derived from other considerations; see V. P. Furnish, *Theology and Ethics in Paul,* Nashville: Abingdon, 1968, pp. 28-43; *idem,* 'Belonging to Christ: A Paradigm for Ethics in First Corinthians', *Interpretation,* 44/2, 1990, p. 151.
25. George Lindbeck, 'Scripture, Consensus, and Community' in R.J. Neuhaus (ed.), *Biblical Interpretation in Crisis,* Grand Rapids: Eerdmans, 1989, pp. 74-101.
26. Gustafson observes that 'the study of the ethics in the Scriptures ... is a complex task for which few are well prepared; those who are specialists in ethics generally lack the intensive and proper training in biblical studies, and those who are specialists in biblical studies often lack sophistication in ethical thought', 'Place of Scripture', p. 430.
27. See, for example, the eleven problems briefly surveyed by I.H. Marshall, 'The Use of the New Testament in Christian Ethics', *Expository Times,* 105/5, 1994, pp. 131-33. See also C.S. Rodd, 'The Use of the Old Testament in Christian Ethics', *Expository Times,* 105/4, 1994, pp. 101-02. A more technical discussion of hermeneutical dilemmas is found in Cahill, *Between the Sexes,* pp. 15-44.
28. There is truth in Fowl and Jones' assertion that 'the most important discontinuities are not historical, but moral and theological. That is, the important discontinuities between Scripture and our contemporary settings are more likely found within us, specifically in our inability and unwillingness to provide and embody wise readings of the texts, than in gaps of historical time', Stephen E. Fowl and L. Gregory Jones, *Reading in Communion,* London: SPCK, 1991, p. 61, also p. 81. See also Hauerwas, 'Moral Authority of Scripture', p. 369f.
29. I.H. Marshall, 'How Do We Interpret The Bible Today?', *Themelios,* 5/2, 1980, p. 10; J. Packer, 'Infallible Scripture and the Role of Hermeneutics' in D.A. Carson and J.D. Woodbridge (eds), *Scripture and Truth,* Leicester: IVP, 1983, p. 331f.
30. For a recent discussion of this with respect to the ethics of Jesus, see A.E. Harvey, *Strenuous Commands: The Ethic of Jesus,* London: SCM, 1990.
31. Swartley, Slavery, Sabbath, War and Women, pp. 217-18.

32. The practice of setting up a canon within a canon is usually rejected in principle by most interpreters. But in practice it seems unavoidable, for the moment we favour New Testament over Old Testament teaching, or differentiate between what is culturally relative and what is abiding revelation, we are effectively setting up a canon within a canon. See Robin Scroggs, 'Can the New Testament Be Relevant for the Twenty-first Century?' in *idem, The Text and the Times,* Minneapolis: Fortress, 1993, pp. 273-75; also J.D.G. Dunn, *The Living Word,* London: SCM, 1987, pp. 44-64, pp. 141-74. In relation to this, Fowl and Jones make a helpful distinction between a normative and functional canon within a canon.
    * A *normative* canon within a canon is where certain texts are excluded from consideration on *a priori* grounds. This is to be rejected outright, for 'no text – no matter how 'difficult' – should be excluded from the ongoing processes of communal discernment in relation to the whole witness of Scripture'.
    * A *functional* canon within a canon is where certain texts are discerned by certain communities at certain times to be more appropriate than others. This is quite acceptable. 'Within a canon as diverse as the one Christians recognise, there is no reason to think that all of its texts will be equally relevant in any given situation. Some texts will be more appropriate than others in any given situation. This sets up a 'functional' canon within a canon'.

    Fowl/Jones, *Reading in Communion,* p. 53, n. 23.
33. Lindbeck, 'Scripture, Consensus, and Community', p. 90. So too Francis Schüssler Fiorenza, 'The Crisis of Scriptural Authority: Interpretation and Reception', *Interpretation,* 44/4, 1990, p. 356f.
34. Lindbeck, 'Scripture, Consensus, and Community', p. 88ff.
35. See Fowl/Jones, *Reading in Communion*, pp. 14-21.
36. Richard B. Hays, 'Scripture-Shaped Community: the Problem of Method in New Testament Ethics', *Interpretation,* 54/1, 1990, p. 43.
37. So C. Freeman Sleeper, 'Ethics as a Context for Biblical Interpretation', *Interpretation,* 22/4, 1968, p. 460; Gustafson, 'Place of Scripture', p. 439; Birch and Rasmussen, *Bible and Ethics,* p. 166f.
38. Cf. Scroggs, 'New Testament and Ethics', p. 90f.
39. James F. Childress, 'Scripture and Christian Ethics: Some Reflections on the Role of Scripture in Moral Deliberation and Justification', *Interpretation,* 34/4, 1980, p. 378. So too William C. Spohn, *What Are They Saying About Scripture and Ethics?,* New York/Ramsey: Paulist Press, 1984, pp. 3, 4, 5, 90.
40. Fowl and Jones, *Reading in Communion*, p. 13.
41. Cf. Long, 'Use of the Bible', pp. 150-52.
42. For the distinction between a revealed morality and a revealed reality, see Gustafson, 'Place of Scripture', pp. 430-55.
43. Of course, this is true of every use of the Bible in ethics; we always relate equivocally or ambiguously to the text, accepting certain parts, rejecting some and qualifying others. The literalist refuses to admit to doing so however.
44. Birch and Rasmussen, *Bible and Ethics,* p. 184.
45. The problem is that when one attempts to take all of Jesus' words this way, one soon discovers many are impossible to keep, so that even the most serious Christian is forced to accept an ethically unsatisfactory compromise. For a brief survey of interpretive

options, see W.D. Davies and D.C. Allison, 'Reflections on the Sermon on the Mount', *Scottish Journal of Theology,* 44/3, 1991, pp. 283-309. According to Furnish, 'Paul nowhere lays down a rigid, legalistic code of Christian conduct', *Moral Teaching,* p. 17.

46. Cf. J. Goldingay, 'Models for Scripture', *Scottish Journal of Theology,* 44/1, 1991, pp. 19-37; *idem,* 'Models of Theological Reflection in the Bible', *Theology,* 759, 1991, pp. 181-88.
47. Furnish has termed this 'the law of varying relevancy' – the more specifically relevant any given moral instruction is to a particular biblical situation, the less specifically relevant it is to other particular situations, *Moral Teaching*, p. 16. In a more recent article, Furnish renamed this 'the law of *diminishing* relevancy' – insofar as counsels were *specifically* applicable in the situations to which they were originally addressed, they *cannot be specifically* applicable in other situations; *idem*, 'Belonging to Christ', p. 146.
48. Cf. Gustafson, 'Place of Scripture', 439f; R.N. Longenecker, *New Testament Social Ethics For Today,* Grand Rapids: Eerdmans, 1984, p. 3.
49. For an excellent discussion on how the New Testament can be used for social ethics, see C. Mott, 'The Use of the Bible in Social Ethics II: The Use of the New Testament', Part I, *Transformation,* 1/2, 1984, pp. 11-20; Part II, *Transformation,* 1/3, 1984, pp. 19-26.
50. Cf. Childress, 'Scripture and Christian Ethics', p. 378ff; Don Mathieson, 'Principles and Rules in Christian Ethics', *Latimer Journal,* 107, 1991, pp. 8-16; D. G. Bloesch, *Freedom for Obedience,* San Francisco: Harper and Rowe, 1987, p. 55f; Longenecker, *New Testament Social Ethics*, p. 14f; B. Ramm, *Protestant Biblical Interpretation,* Grand Rapids: Baker, 1970, p. 179f.
51. For example, 'Do not do anything that causes your brother or sister to stumble' (1 Cor 8:13; Rom 14:13-21); 'Keep your life free from the love of money and be content with what you have' (Heb 13:5); 'Do not be unequally yoked together with unbelievers' (2 Cor 6:14); 'Do all things decently and in order; for God is not a God of confusion but peace' (1 Cor 14:35).
52. For example, the ban on charging interest in Old Testament law (Ex 22:25; Lev 25:36; Deut 23:19), in the context of primitive agrarian society, expresses the principle that 'it is wrong to exploit the poor'. In our modern, commercial, inflationary society, charging interest may be acceptable as long as it does not violate this principle.
53. Marshall, 'Using the Bible in Ethics', p. 51; *idem,* 'Use of the New Testament', p.133, p.135f.
54. See especially Longenecker's 'developmental' hermeneutic in *New Testament Social Ethics;* also D. P. Fuller, 'Paul and Galatians 3:28', *TSF Bulletin,* 9, 1985, pp. 9-13.
55. For a recent example, see Terrance Tiessen, 'Toward a Hermeneutic for Discerning Universal Moral Absolutes', *Journal of the Evangelical Theological Society,* 36/2, 1993, pp. 189-207.
56. Harvey points out that although the ethic of Jesus has been generally recognized to have made a distinctive contribution to the moral development of the West, Jesus' ethic has been greatly neglected, both in everyday practice and in Christian moral philosophy; *Strenuous Commands*, esp. Chaps. 1, 2, and 9.
57. R.A. Horsely, 'Ethics and Exegesis: "Love Your Enemies" and the Doctrine of Non-

Violence', *Journal of the American Academy of Religion,* 54, 1986, p. 4. Cf. Yoder, 'Hermeneutics of Peoplehood', pp. 59-61.

58. Michael Schluter and Roy Clements, 'Jubilee Institutional Norms: A Middle Way between Creation Ethics and Kingdom Ethics as the Basis for Christian Political Action', *Evangelical Quarterly,* 62/1, 1990, p. 49.
59. For example, Mathieson suggests that many items of Paul's teaching (on gender, on work, on disputes between believers) imply the principle of doing nothing to bring the church into avoidable public contempt by deliberately flouting conventional secular morality; 'Principles and Rules', p. 10.
60. So Schluter and Clements, 'Jubilee Institutional Norms', p. 49. Such a pattern is often sought either in the social life of ancient Israel or Jesus' proclamation of the kingdom of God. See, for example, Chris Wright, *The Use of the Bible in Social Ethics,* Bramcote, Notts: Grove Books, 1983; Bruce Kaye, *Using the Bible in Ethics,* Bramcote Notts: Grove Books, 1976; Oliver R. Barclay and Chris Sugden, 'Biblical Social Ethics in a Mixed Society', *Evangelical Quarterly,* 62/1, 1990, pp. 5-18; Oliver Barclay, 'The Theology of Social Ethics: A Survey of Current Positions', *Interchange,* 36, 1985, pp. 6-23.
61. See Jonathan Boston, 'Moral Dilemmas and the Problems of Compromise: Two Christian Perspectives', *Stimulus,* 1/3, 1993, pp. 2-12; *idem,* 'Sinning Boldly: Helmut Thielicke's Approach to Ethical Compromise and Borderline Situations', *Crux* 29/2, 1993, pp. 7-17.
62. Childress, 'Scripture and Christian Ethics', p. 380; Spohn, *Scripture and Ethics*, p. 135.
63. Cf. Spohn, *Scripture and Ethics*, pp. 19-35.
64. Ibid., p. 82.
65. Spohn identifies several criteria implicit in Niebuhr's use of Scripture: (i) Those biblical images that function as continuing sources of revelation for the biblical tradition (e.g. the exodus) are most appropriate; (ii) guiding images should be consistent with a theologically sound image of God; (iii) images should be consistent with God's definitive revelation in Jesus Christ; images from both testaments must be gauged against the story of Jesus; (iv) images should be appropriate to the situation addressed and shed light upon it; (v) the images used should indicate courses of action that concur with the standards of ordinary human morality. *Scripture and Ethics*, p. 83f.
66. See J.H. Yoder, 'Withdrawal and Diaspora: The Two faces of Liberation', in Daniel S. Schipani (ed.), *Freedom and Discipleship,* Maryknoll NY: Orbis, 1989, pp. 76-84.
67. Cf. James M. Gustafson, 'The Relation of the Gospels to the Moral Life' in D.G. Miller and D.Y. Hadidan, *Jesus and Man's Hope,* Pittsburgh: Pittsburgh Theological Seminary, 1971, II, pp. 111-116.
68. E. Schüssler-Fiorenza, *In Memory of Her,* London: SCM, 1983, pp. 33-34. As Perkins observes, 'the interrelationship between our experiences of the demands of justice and love in our context and the exhortations of the Bible are quite different if we perceive the latter as structuring prototype rather than definitive archetype', in 'New Testament Ethics: Questions and Contexts', *Religious Studies Review,* 10/4, 1984, p. 325.
69. See Fowl/Jones, *Reading in Communion*, pp. 57-65.
70. It is generally accepted that 'typology' best expresses the way the New Testament

writers handle Old Testament Scripture. It is worth noting, however, that typology is employed throughout the Old Testament as well as in the New Testament. For example, the *Exodus* is the supreme example of God's saving activity in the Old Testament, and thus is frequently treated as a typical event by other biblical writers, both in Old Testament (e.g. Pss 66,77,135,136; Hos 11; Isa 63:11-14) and New Testament (1 Cor 10:1-11; Rev 15:1-8). Sometimes *David* serves as a type of how other believers should live (1 Kgs 3;14; 15:3,11; cf. Ezek 34:24; Zech 12:8; Matt 12:3-4; Heb 11:32). On the other hand, *Cain* (1 Jn 3:12; Jude 11) and the stubborn *Israelites in the wilderness* (Ps 95:8-11; Heb 3:7-4:11) are examples not to be imitated. Again, *Zion* is sometimes used to refer to the holy city built on the hill of Zion (Ps 97:8; Isa 28:16), and thence becomes a type of the spiritual home of all who belong to true Israel (Isa 60:14; Mic 4:1-2; Heb 12:22; 1 Pet 2:5-6; Rev 14:1). For other typological connections, cf. Num 21:4-9 with 2 Kg 18:4; Jn 3;14-16; 1 Cor 10. The Old Testament prophets, rather than giving a photographic outline of the future, usually describe the future in terms of what happened in the past (e.g. Isa 44-66 describes the deliverance from Babylon in terms of a second exodus, and even employs imagery drawn from creation, Noahic stories, the flood narrative and Abraham's call). This means that the prophets used past history *typologically* – historical events were a type of how God would act eschatologically.

71. Scroggs, 'Can the New Testament Be Relevant', p. 276. Cf. his earlier, more positive appeal to analogy in 'New Testament and Ethics', p. 93.
72. Horsely, 'Ethics and Exegesis', p. 4.
73. Ibid., p. 26.
74. So Gustafson, 'Place of Scripture', p. 443; Horsely, 'Ethics and Exegesis', p. 4, p. 25f.
75. Lisa Sowle Cahill, 'The New Testament and Ethics: Communities of Social Change', *Interpretation,* 44/4, 1990, p. 384
76. Fowl/Jones, *Reading in Communion*, p. 9.
77. Cf. Scroggs, 'Can the New Testament Be Relevant', pp. 280-85.
78. For this distinction, see Stephen Westerholm, *Israel's Law and the Church's Faith,* Grand Rapids: Eerdmans, 1988, pp. 201-05.
79. McGrath, 'Doctrine and Ethics', p. 152.
80. See Birch and Rasmussen, *Bible and Ethics,* pp. 62-65, pp. 189-94.
81. Spohn, *Scripture and Ethics,* p. 127.
82. Cf. J W. Thompson, 'The Ethics of Jesus and the Early Church', in Perry Cotham (ed.), *Christian Social Ethics,* Grand Rapids: Baker, 1979, p. 58.
83. Cf. Wayne A. Meeks, 'Understanding Early Christian Ethics', *Journal of Biblical Literature,* 105/1, 1986, p. 4ff.
84. Cahill, 'New Testament and Ethics', p. 384f. Schüssler Fiorenza proposes that the Scriptures provide the basic constitution of the community, consisting not of a set of laws but 'a set of interpretive principles that provide basic paradigms of Christian identity', 'Crisis of Scriptural Authority', p. 364.
85. In his important recent study, R. B. Hays stresses the 'eclessiocentric' as well as Christocentic nature of Paul's interpretation of Scripture, *Echoes of Scripture in the Letters of Paul,* New Haven and London: Yale University Press, 1989.
86. Yoder, 'Hermeneutics of Peoplehood', 50-56; cf. Birch and Rasmussen, *Bible and Ethics*, pp. 108-11.

87. Cf. Hauerwas, 'Moral Authority of Scripture', pp. 356-63; Birch and Rasmussen, *Bible and Ethics,* p. 145ff.
88. Wayne A. Meeks, 'A Hermeneutics of Social Embodiment', *Harvard Theological Review,* 79/1-3, 1986, pp. 183f.
89. Cahill, 'New Testament and Ethics', p. 393.
90. Cf. B.C. Ollenberger, 'The Hermeneutics of Obedience' in W. M. Swartley (ed.), *Essays on Biblical Interpretation,* Elkhart, IN: Institute of Mennonite Studies, 1984, pp. 45-61.
91. Fowl/Jones, *Reading in Communion,* p. 20.
92. C.D. Marshall, *Faith as a Theme in Mark's Narrative,* Cambridge: CUP, 1989, p. 27.
93. Birch and Rasmussen, *Bible and Ethics,* 127, cf. pp. 105-07.
94. For examples of such an approach, see Richard Lischer, 'The Sermon on the Mount as Radical Pastoral Care', *Interpretation,* 41, 1987, pp. 157-69. Stanley Hauerwas, 'The Sermon on the Mount, Just War and the Quest for Peace', *Concilium,* 215, 1988, pp. 36-43.
95. See C.D. Marshall, *Kingdom Come. The Kingdom of God in the Teaching of Jesus,* Auckland: Impetus, 1993, pp. 76-93.
96. Hays, 'Scripture-Shaped Community', p. 51.
97. For a recent evaluation of Yoder's contribution, see Joel Zimbelman, 'The Contribution of John Howard Yoder to Recent Discussions in Christian Social Ethics', *Scottish Journal of Theology,* 45, 1992, pp. 367-99.
98. See the discussion in Yoder, 'Hermeneutics of Peoplehood', pp. 61-64.
99. See Cahill, 'New Testament and Ethics', p. 384.
100. Fowl/Jones, *Reading in Communion,* pp. 44-49, pp. 110-34.
101. It would be a mistake to divorce the distinctive communal character of early Christian faith from its eschatological or apocalyptic character. When both features are seen as inseparable, it becomes impossible to use the New Testament to justify a sectarian retreat from the world. See A.N. Wilder, 'Kerygma, Eschatology and Social Ethics' in W.D. Davies and D. Daube (eds), *The Background of the New Testament and Its Eschatology,* Cambridge: CUP, 1964, pp. 509-36; John A. Henley, 'Eschatology and Community in the Ethics of Paul', *ABR* 27, 1979, pp. 24-44; and especially Nancy Duff, 'The Significance of Pauline Apocalyptic for Theological Ethics' in J. Marcus and M.L. Soards (eds), *Apocalyptic and the New Testament,* Sheffield: JSOT, 1989, pp. 279-96.
102. Fowl/Jones, *Reading in Communion,* p. 64.
103. Cahill, 'New Testament and Ethics', p. 394.
104. According to Meeks, 'The judgement that the controlling pattern is, or ought to be, narrative does not emerge either from a tabulation of actual uses or from a compilation of the different genres found within the canon', in 'Hermeneutics of Social Embodiment', p. 185. For Hauerwas, however, the fact that Scripture contains much material that is not narrative in character does not undermine the priority of story, since such material, so far as it is Scripture, gains its intelligibility by being a product of and contribution to the wider story, which the community lives through remembering. Also, 'one of the virtues of calling attention to the narrative nature of Scripture is the way it releases us

from making unsupportable claims about the unity of Scripture or the centrality of the 'biblical view of X or Y", in 'Moral Authority of Scripture', p. 366.
105. Yoder, 'Hermeneutics of Peoplehood', p. 57.
106. Birch and Rasmussen, *Bible and Ethics,* p. 204 n.3, cf. pp. 114-17.
107. Yoder, 'Hermeneutics of Peoplehood', p. 58. Cf. the synthesis of the traditional juridical style of ethical reasoning and koinonia ethics advocated by Birch and Rasmussen, *Bible and Ethics,* pp. 108-119.
108. See R.H. Fuller, 'The Decalogue in the New Testament', *Interpretation,* 43/3, 1989, pp. 243-55.
109. See W.D. Davies, 'The Relevance of the Moral Teaching of the Early Church' in E. Earle Ellis and Max Wilcox (eds), *Neotestamentica et Semitica,* Edinburgh: T and T Clark, 1969, pp. 35-38.
110. So also Hays, 'Scripture Shaped Community', p. 49; Childress, 'Scripture and Christian Ethics', p. 378.

Chapter 5

Catholic Social Teaching

A Rich Heritage

Ruth Smithies

Introduction

The main principles in the church leaders' *Social Justice Statement* have been identified and discussed in earlier chapters. This chapter explores their origins and examines the context in which they were advanced. In particular, it notes the strong parallels between the principles enunciated in the *Statement* and the central themes of Catholic Social Teaching (CST).

The Catholic Church has developed an extensive body of documents on economic, social and political matters expressing a consistent set of ideas. These ideas include:

- the pre-eminence of human dignity, with its concomitant rights and responsibilities
- the belief that human persons are social beings and that their God-given nature calls them to live in community
- the importance of the concepts of the common good, subsidiarity and solidarity
- the essential place of work
- the preferential option for the poor.

These very same ideas appear in the headings of the church leaders' *Social Justice Statement*. They are summed up in §.6 of the *Statement* and occur again in §§.11-13, 18-19, 26-30, 36-38, and 41-42. It is not unreasonable to conclude that the specific contribution made by the Catholic Church to the Social Justice Initiative was its sharing with the other churches of the rich heritage of CST.

This chapter describes this heritage in the hope that it will illuminate an important part of the background to the *Statement*. The chapter begins by exploring the purpose, sources and development of CST. It then considers the views of CST on social justice, the common good and the role of the state. Although there is an extensive literature on CST, I have chosen to refer almost exclusively to the original teaching documents rather than secondary sources. This is because the primary sources need to be read if one wishes to gain an accurate understanding of CST.

What is CST?

CST is that part of Catholic moral teaching which deals with the nature of moral behaviour in the social, political and economic order. It is the application of Catholic moral theology to the ethical questions raised by human societies, institutions and structures. CST affirms that the world should not be rejected. The church cannot be reduced to a spiritual model. Christianity is not a call to move away from the world into a privatised faith limited to a personal relationship with God. It is not simply a call to save one's soul in a sinful world. It is also a call to be fully alive to, and engage with, the world.

But living in a complex world and knowing what to do as Christians is not always easy; hence the need for guidance. CST indicates directions to be taken for the just resolution of conflict in a complex world.[1] CST is not so much a theory; it is more a response to the reality in which people, communities and countries find themselves. As moral teaching it is a basis and motivation for action.[2] It aims to enable those who accept it to analyse social, economic and political realities and to make judgements about them.

The premise of CST is that specific, concrete human situations (in other words, *this* world) are important. Quoting the Apostle Paul who warned Christians not to be 'conformed to this world',[3] the Second Vatican Council wrote that Paul's call is not a rejection of this world but a call not to take on 'that spirit of vanity and malice which transforms into an instrument of sin those human energies intended for the service of God and people'.[4] This quote comes from one of the four Pastoral Constitutions, known as the *Pastoral Constitution on the Church in the Modern World* (*Gaudium et Spes*). This is generally considered to be the most authoritative writing in the corpus of CST documents. It deals with the relationship between the church and the world. It states that the City of God exists side by side with the secular city. The two cities interpenetrate one another.[5] The shape of this world will pass away.[6] But 'the expectation of a new heaven and a new earth must not weaken but rather stimulate our concern for this earth'.[7] Further, 'While earthly progress must be carefully distinguished from the growth of God's kingdom, to the extent that the former can contribute to the better ordering of human society, it is of vital concern to the Kingdom of God'.[8] In this way human society and the Kingdom of God are related. While teaching that the Kingdom of God is not exhausted by human and time-bound arrangements, the CST documents insist that the Kingdom of God is not a spiritual world separate from this one. The Kingdom is already brought about here and now, not just at the end of time.

It needs to be stressed that CST documents are moral teaching and do not aim to espouse a political or economic theory. They do not favour either capitalism or socialism, nor a 'middle way' between the two. While CST is not a political, economic or social doctrine, it has an interdisciplinary dimension. The documents state that the Church wants to listen to what other disciplines such as economics, sociology, and political science have to contribute and to attempt to make these disciplines seek a broader horizon aimed at serving human beings.[9]

CST documents have consistently condemned communism and socialism for their atheism and view of the human person as submerged in the larger structure. To give a recent example, Pope John Paul II said in September 1993:

> Deprived of a transcendent reference, human beings become little more than a drop in the ocean, and their dignity, no matter how sincerely acknowledged and proclaimed, loses its most solid guarantee. Thus it happened that, in the name of 'class', or of a presumed benefit for society, individuals were oppressed and even eliminated.[10]

CST has equally distanced itself from liberalism and capitalism, holding them responsible for grave social injustices; it has also rejected capitalism's view on freedom. In another address in 1993, Pope John Paul II commented:

> The Church has vigorously raised her voice against the corruption of freedom, in both the political and economic spheres. In this regard, ever since Leo XIII's *Rerum Novarum* not only socialism but also economic liberalism, that scorns every limitation and is unconcerned about the demands of solidarity, has been condemned.[11]

The purpose of CST is to guide human behaviour. Therefore, it has been problem-oriented and has evolved with the changing social, economic and political questions and problems of concrete situations. It has not done this by providing blueprints and has explicitly rejected drawing up a programme of specific policies. Concerned about God's plan for people and creation, it has been interested in the moral implications of economics and politics, not in their technical or organisational aspects. To quote Pope John Paul II again: 'Catholic Social Teaching's main aim is to interpret the complex realities of human existence, determining their conformity with or divergence from the lines of the Gospel teaching on people and their vocation'.[12]

Though the aim of CST is to interpret complex realities, the contents of CST are principles. Interpretation and application of the principles is up to the various Christian communities. Pope Paul VI in an encyclical in 1971 wrote: 'It is up to the Christian communities to analyse with objectivity the situation which is proper to their own country, to shed on it the light of the Gospel's unalterable words and to draw principles of reflection, norms of judgements and directives for action from the social teaching of the Church'.[13]

This is where problems can arise: because CST is essentially theology, and particularly moral theology, it has not offered 'technical' solutions or concrete policies. It has left the practical application of the principles to the Christian communities. Technical solutions are primarily the responsibility of Christians working through the state and other institutions in society. At the same time, CST has acknowledged that:

> The transition from theory to practice is of its very nature difficult; and it is especially so when one tries to reduce to concrete terms a social doctrine such as that of the Church. There are several reasons why this is so; among them we can mention people's deep-rooted selfishness ....[14]

This can lead to different opinions:

> Differences in the application of principles can sometimes arise, even among sincere Catholics. When this happens they should be careful not to lose their respect and esteem for each other. Instead they should strive to find points of agreement for effective and suitable action, and not wear themselves out in interminable arguments, and under pretext of the better or the best, omit to do the good that is possible and therefore obligatory.[15]

Yet for those familiar with the CST documents it is obvious that they have done much more than provide principles. The documents have analysed, applied and given directives for action on a very wide range of topics – from the arms race to democracy, from trade unions to the United Nations, from development aid to the market economy.

Origins and Sources of CST

It is common in recent times to hear of the hundred years of CST and to have the encyclical *Rerum Novarum*, written by Pope Leo XIII in 1891, referred to as the first social encyclical. This encyclical was indeed the first papal letter written for the sole purpose of addressing the social, political and economic questions of the time. But questions of social ethics and how to respond to them did not emerge only a hundred years ago.

With the spread of Christianity throughout Europe came a deep penetration of the Christian ethos in all aspects of social life: marriage, family, education, government, commerce, and economic life. Christian values influenced deeply the practice of law, justice and jurisprudence and inspired important legal codes. In the crafts, trades and professions Christian teaching was felt on the questions of contracts, wages, loans, interest and prices. Thomas Aquinas was one of the first Christian thinkers to treat questions of social ethics in a systematic way, especially in his *Summa Theologica* on the problems of justice and law. During the fifteenth century several social documents from the Popes of that period began to appear which also dealt with issues such as the slave trade, branded as 'a great crime' by Pius II (1462). The problem of usury was treated often. Pope Paul III with his letter *Veritas Ipsa* (1537) strongly defended the dignity of the indigenous people threatened by the colonisation of the New World.[16]

But it was the industrial revolution and attraction of Marxist solutions which moved the Catholic Church to issue its first social encyclical. The encyclical letter *Rerum Novarum* (1891) constituted a new approach. Through a dialogue with the new industrial world the Catholic Church was making a direct appeal to the people and to all interested parties; it did not limit itself to reminding the civil authorities of their responsibilities. It presented its view on the social problems of the time and formulated principles which it believed would lead to just solutions. *Rerum Novarum* was drafted with the help of a team of international specialists and it incorporated the results of many years of social thought. This too became a feature of subsequent social encyclicals.

In *Rerum Novarum* Pope Leo XIII called the attention of the world to the undeserved misery of so many people. He wrote: 'Some opportune remedy must be found quickly for the misery and wretchedness pressing so unjustly on the majority of the working class'.[17] The Catholic Church, he claimed, had the moral authority to promote justice; the state had the obligation, through legislation, to protect the workers and defend the rights of associations. The state's role was a suppletive one. The associations, formed of workers and industrialists, together or separately, were the proper means to protect the interests of all parties and especially of the poor.

Forty years after *Rerum Novarum*, Pope Pius XI published the encyclical *Quadragesimo Anno* in May 1931. This encyclical expanded the doctrine of Leo XII and discussed the then burning issues of economic concentration, unemployment, the intervention of the state, the role of labour unions, the individual and social character of private property, the class struggle and the autocratic abuse of state power.

Reconstructing the social order, the Pope stated, will require the harmonious co-operation of all classes acting in the spirit of justice and charity. Having stressed the principle of subsidiarity, whereby each level in society should be able to deal with its own problems, Pius XI vindicated with caution and firmness the legitimacy of state intervention in the economic sphere:

> Free competition, and especially economic domination, must be kept within definite and proper bounds, and must be brought under effective control of the public authority, in matters pertaining to the latter's competence. The public institutions of the nations should be such as to make all human society conform to the requirements of the common good, that is, the norm of social justice.[18]

The term 'common good' had already been used by Pope Leo XIII, but the appearance of the term 'social justice' is a first in the CST tradition. What those matters are which 'pertain to the competence of the public authority' is dealt with in *Quadragesimo Anno* in the context of property rights: 'Provided that the natural and divine law be observed, the public authority, in view of the common good, may specify more accurately what is licit and what is illicit for property owners in the use of their possessions.'[19]

From the 1960s onwards it became customary to commemorate every tenth anniversary of *Rerum Novarum*. On the seventieth anniversary Pope John XXIII published the encyclical *Mater et Magistra* (1961). The encyclical reaffirmed the teaching of his predecessors, but new aspects included the role of private and public initiatives and the trend towards socialisation (understood in the sense of greater interdependence and mutual responsibility). The encyclical also looked at the just wages of workers and their role in the structure of the enterprises, the social and economic aspects of development, and the growing role of women in society.

The subsequent anniversary encyclical *Octogesima Adveniens* (1971) called for effective action:

> If the role of the hierarchy is to teach and to interpret authentically the norms of morality to be followed in this matter, it belongs to the laity, without waiting passively for orders and directives, to take the initiative freely and to infuse a Christian spirit into the mentality, customs, laws and structures of the community in which they live. Let each one examine himself, to see what he has done up to now, and what he ought to do. It is not enough to recall principles, state intentions, point to crying injustices and utter prophetic denunciations; these words will lack real weight unless they are accompanied for each individual by a livelier awareness of personal responsibility and by effective action.[20]

Laborem Exercens (1981) considered the meaning and central place of work for people. Finally, *Centesimus Annus* (1991) called for a society which respects the true freedom and dignity of the human person.

All the encyclicals mentioned are substantive documents. *Centesimus Annus*, for example, is over 50 pages. All the encyclicals, but especially the later ones, deal with a large number of issues, often in some detail. In a short chapter of this nature it is impossible to even approach a fair coverage of their contents.

Not all of what constitutes CST is written by Popes. Since 1963 a large number of social teaching documents have been issued by the teaching authority of the church. There is, as mentioned, the Second Vatican Council document *Gaudium et Spes*. There are also the many authoritative documents issued by regional and national Bishops' Conferences. Examples include the Medellin Conference documents issued by the Latin American Episcopal Conference in 1968 and the Pastoral Letter of the United States Bishops on the US Economy in 1986. These documents apply the major principles of CST to local circumstances. A recent example of the development of CST in this part of the world is *Common Wealth for the Common Good* issued in 1992 by the Australian Bishops' Conference. This deals, amongst other things, with the distribution of wealth in Australia. It is probably legitimate to include the New Zealand church leaders' *Social Justice Statement* in the list of CST documents: it is co-signed by the Archbishop of Wellington who as Archbishop is part of, and represents, the teaching authority in the Catholic Church.

The Development of CST

None of the encyclicals in the long series from *Rerum Novarum* (1891) to *Centesimus Annus* (1991) attempted to give a complete vision on all issues faced by society. Rather, each one endeavoured to respond to some particular issues of the time. This is one reason why CST is not static but is continually developing. Another reason is the expanding geographical horizon. The earlier encyclicals were written in a European context; increasingly they have taken on a global perspective. The key developments in CST can be summarised as follows.

1. From Inductive to Deductive

The earlier encyclicals based their teaching more on the tradition of early writers and especially the scholastic philosophy of Thomas Aquinas in which the concept of natural law is central. The doctrine of natural law is based on the belief that humans flourish if they exercise their freedom according to the law inscribed in their heart by God.[21] Natural law as understood in the Catholic tradition refers to the reality that within the consciences of all human beings there are non-conventional, non-arbitrary moral standards. This is the law inscribed in everyone's heart; it gives true moral knowledge even for those who have not received the moral instruction of divine revelation.

From the 1960s onwards, signalling the more pronounced affirmation of the importance of the Bible, the encyclicals have drawn more directly on revelation and the biblical vision of a God of mercy and justice, who calls people and communities to act justly. The trend in the encyclicals has been to reflect on what is happening in the world and reflect on the lived experience of the 'people of God' who struggle to be faithful to the call for justice and mercy. In this way the encyclicals have become more deductive in their approach. They have attempted to read the 'signs of the time' in the awareness of the merciful plan of the God of the Old and New Testament who acts within history.[22]

2. *From Eurocentric to Global*

The earlier encyclicals were written in the context of European events and focused on issues which were a direct result of industrialisation. It was *Mater et Magistra* (1961) which internationalised CST by treating situations in countries not fully industrialised. The encyclical discussed the problems of the agricultural sector and those caused by urbanisation.

From this encyclical onwards CST has a global perspective, both in geographical terms (moving outside of Europe) and in cultural terms. The Second Vatican Council was in fact the first Council to reflect truly a multicultural dimension. Following the missionary efforts of the nineteenth and early twentieth centuries, the Catholic Church had to a degree become incarnate in cultures other than European. Also, in the 1950s and 1960s large numbers of former colonies regained their independence. The encyclicals have become more global in a third sense: from Pope John XXIII onwards the encyclicals are addressed not only to Catholics but also to 'all people of goodwill'.

3. *From East/West to North/South*

With the globalisation of CST came a shift away from the tension between the capitalist and socialist 'blocs' (i.e. the tension between East and West) to the tension within countries and between countries of the 'haves' and 'have-nots' (i.e. the tension between North and South). Most Catholics had seen the church's social teaching as a bulwark against communism and interpreted the cause of the West as the cause of the Catholic Church. Thus, the curious situation had arisen that many Catholics in the West – wrongly as it happens – did not consider themselves challenged by CST. Such complacency was no longer possible with the increasing focus on the unjust distribution of resources particularly between the rich countries in the North (the so-called developed world) and the underdeveloped nations of the South.

4. *Widening the Concept of Sin*

The Catholic Church has always understood it to be its duty to denounce individuals for their unjust behaviour: kings, legislators, owners, employers. But the later encyclicals have a clearer perception not only of individual, but also of corporate responsibility. Since the 1970s the encyclicals no longer denounced only unjust acts, but also structural disorders engendering collective injustice, violence, exploitation. These are called 'structures of sin'. They are rooted in personal sin. They are linked to concrete acts of individuals who introduce these structures, consolidate them and make them difficult to remove. Thus they grow stronger and spread and become a source of other sins and so influence people's behaviour.[23] Pope John Paul II defined structures of sin as 'the sum total of factors which work against the achievements of the common good and respect for human dignity'.[24]

5. *Widening the Concept of Poverty*

Rerum Novarum was a response to the terrible conditions of material deprivation to which the new and often violent process of industrialisation had reduced large numbers of people. All later encyclicals have continued to speak out against exploitation and for the fulfilment of the material needs of all human beings. For example, the anniversary encyclical *Centesimus Annus* pointed out that in many parts of the world similar processes of transformation have contributed to hunger and starvation.[25]

The later encyclicals have pointed out that in addition to lacking material goods, the world's poor also lack the less tangible but equally important goods of knowledge, education and know-how. The poor do not have the opportunities to enter the network of knowledge and communications which would enable them to see their qualities appreciated and utilised. Thus, if not actually exploited they are to a great extent marginalised. The encyclicals have drawn attention to the existence of the poor in the rich countries where vast groups of people are both materially poor and as well as marginalised, that is they are educationally poor, lacking knowledge, training and opportunities.[26]

A third form of poverty is also mentioned in the later encyclicals: spiritual poverty. This is most visible in the materialistic and hedonistic, consumption- and pleasure-oriented lifestyles of many people in First World countries. In this poverty people become alienated from each other and from their own true selves. They try to fill their spiritual poverty with substitutes such as drugs and pornography.[27]

6. *Preferential Option for the Poor: A Call to Justice*

Concern for those people who are especially beloved to Jesus, the poor, the hungry and the rejected, is part of the Christian tradition. It is also found in all CST documents, starting with *Rerum Novarum* which declared that its purpose was to find 'a remedy for the misery and wretchedness of the working class'.[28] It is this concern which is expressed in the phrase 'preferential option for the poor': The deprivation and powerlessness of the poor wounds the whole community. In accordance with God's own revelation as the Liberator of the oppressed and the Defender of the poor, a preferential love should be shown to the poor. Pope John Paul II defined it 'as a special form of primacy in the exercise of Christian charity'.[29]

The earlier encyclicals held that it was a duty of charity for the rich to give to the poor. While the emphasis on *duty* has remained, the later encyclicals have expanded the understanding of why the rich should give to the poor: they should also give in order to meet the demands of *justice*: The poor have a *right* to share in the enjoyment of material goods because God created the earth for everyone. God did not intend to exclude anyone or favour anyone. It is therefore not only a question of the rich giving from their surplus to the poor (charity), but justice demands that the poor are enabled to get their rightful share of the earth's goodness.[30] The share is called 'rightful' because God has given each person the right to share in the goods of the earth. For the rich this implies a change in lifestyle.[31]

CST, Social Justice and the Common Good

The church leaders issued the *Social Justice Statement* to reflect their deep concern for social justice (§.2). In §.3 the *Statement* defines social justice as fairness in all relationships and structures. How does this definition compare with CST?

First, the terms 'justice' and 'social justice' are used in CST documents in a flexible fashion, sometimes interchangeably. Where Scriptural influence is strong, as for example in the Statement emanating from the Synod of Bishops in 1971 entitled *Justice in the World*, the unmodified 'justice' is used.

Second, CST documents have not provided a precise definition for either term. As noted, the term social justice appeared for the first time in *Quadragesimo Anno*: 'Human societies should be confirmed to the requirements of the common good; that is to the norm of social justice'.[32] Exactly what is meant by the term 'social justice' is not spelled out, but in this and subsequent CST documents the concepts of love, social justice and the common good are closely linked. Love is the motivating force: social justice, on the one hand, and charity, on the other, are its concrete expressions. The two expressions are complementary: charity is a reactive expression of love, social justice a proactive one.

The requirements of the common good entail that social justice provide the central thrust toward organising the institutions of a social and juridical order. Social justice is the call to organise a just society; this encompasses primarily commutative and distributive justice. Social justice is not only to be applied to the systems, structures and institutions of society but to all interactions.

It is, therefore, entirely consistent with CST that the *Social Justice Statement* did not only ask for social justice to be expressed in structures and policies of political parties, but also in the behaviour of each and every Christian. This aspect of the *Social Justice Statement* has, in my opinion, received insufficient attention. It is highly significant that the very first question asked by the church leaders is addressed not to institutions or the state but to church members: 'Do you experience New Zealand society as a fair one, and does your way of life contribute to the development of a just society?' (§.5).

Both the definition of the term social justice and the very use of the term in the *Social Justice Statement* have been criticised. In my view, the church leaders were justified in using the term 'social justice' rather than 'justice'. For many New Zealanders the word justice has negative connotations and conjures up images of courts, laws and regulations. In such a climate the use of the word justice could well have been counter-productive. By using the term social justice the church leaders distinguished the common perception of justice from the justice talked about in the Christian tradition which is a reflection of the justice of God. God's justice is linked with salvation. It is not vindictive but salvific. Similarly, in the CST tradition, social justice is every action which promotes the common good.

The Common Good

Social justice and the common good are closely linked concepts in CST. Social justice aims at the realisation of the common good. Anyone who does this displays the virtue of solidarity, defined by Pope John Paul II as 'a firm and persevering determination to commit oneself to the common good'.[33]

What is meant by the common good and how is the common good determined? According to CST, determining what is the common good involves an assessing of the sum total of particular interests 'on the basis of a balanced hierarchy of values; ultimately it demands a correct understanding of the dignity and the rights of the person'.[34] *Gaudium et Spes* defined the common good as 'those conditions of social life which allow social groups and their individual members relatively thorough and ready access to their own fulfilment'.[35] Because the Catholic tradition advocates the common good, at first glance it appears similar to utilitarianism. But in CST the common good is not simply the 'greatest net good' of utilitarian theory. Institutions exist for people and individuals may not be harmed in order that others may prosper or that 'the system' may work. The common good is grounded in God's intentions for the human race; this keeps the common good from being smothered either by individualism or by 'the greater number'. God's intentions for the human race are, among other things, expressed in human nature.

Human Nature

Essential to CST is the belief that the person and society are not in opposition. Although the value of society comes from the value of the human person, human nature as created by God is essentially such that people are relational beings. In this way people reflect the inner life of the Triune God. The interdependence of people calls for solidarity. Freedom is the freedom to exist for others in a sincere giving of self. Only when people are true to their essential nature are they fully and truly free. Thus, an understanding of the Catholic view on human nature is a prerequisite to understanding the Catholic view on social justice and the common good. To quote John Paul II: 'From this vision of the human person flows the correct vision of society and of economic, social and political systems'.[36]

CST and the State

The Catholic tradition does not ground the origin of the state on human sinfulness which would require the power and coercion of the state in order to prevent sinful human beings from destroying one another. Neither does the state exist merely on the basis of a contract made by individuals. Rather, the political community is an organic whole and is based on human nature as described above: people are created as interdependent beings.

CST documents proceed from the view that the political community and public authority are founded on human nature and hence belong to the order designed by God.[37] In other words, in the Catholic tradition the active element that obtains and directs the co-operation of the members is not an external principle, such as the ruler or the perception of the majority that it is in their own interests. The active element that makes the state a reality is that people are made by God in such a way that they are social and therefore political beings. In CST the political community has a distinctive communal end: it exists in order to pursue and fulfil the common good. This is its full justification and meaning, as well as the source of its specific and basic right to exist.[38] The link between the common good and the state is not accidental but intrinsic.[39] The common good should be the primary principle governing the state's activities and it is the task of the state to direct the energies of all its citizens towards the common good.[40]

Human Rights and Duties

In CST human rights and duties are intimately linked with the common good. Immediately after defining the common good, *Gaudium et Spes* continued:

> At the same time, however, there is a growing awareness of the exalted dignity proper to the human person, since he stands above all things and his rights and duties are universal and inviolable. Therefore there must be made available to all people everything necessary for leading a life truly human.[41]

The document continued by spelling out in some detail what these rights are. These rights are both negative and positive rights. Because the state exists for the common good, it has the duty to protect and guarantee human rights and promote human duties.

The Christmas broadcast of Pope Pius XII in 1942 had already offered a broad compendium of the rights of persons and the principles for a just social order. Nearly all CST documents have listed human rights; the lists are not always the same and usually are not complete. The most complete and systematic treatment and listing of human rights is found in the encyclical *Pacem in Terris* by Pope John XXIII in 1963.

The defence of human rights in CST is not a response to humanistic or secular thinking on rights. While the United Nations Declaration on Human Rights is mentioned explicitly as a positive 'sign of the times',[42] the apex of all rights in CST is the right and duty to live in the truth of one's faith and in conformity with one's transcendent dignity as a person.[43] The Catholic Church has linked its defence of human rights directly to its spiritual mission: human rights must be defended and promoted because they are a necessary part of the recognition that must be given to the dignity of the human person created in the image of God and redeemed by Christ.

The CST documents have not addressed directly the question whether rights are unlimited. In my view the answer from the CST documents would run along the following lines. Humans have rights on account of their God-given human dignity. In theory, individual rights and the common good are never in opposition to each other. Human rights are to serve the common good; they are unlimited as long as they do so. If there is a conflict between different rights, it is the right which best expresses and realises the common good which has pre-eminence.

Subsidiarity and Solidarity

In CST the primary principle of the actions of the state is to help realise the common good. This is done is through acting in accordance with two principles, depending on the circumstances: the principle of subsidiarity and the principle of solidarity.[44]

As guardian of the common good the state is charged to safeguard the rights of all, especially the poor and defenceless. To quote Pope John Paul in *Centesimus Annus*:

> The more that individuals are defenceless within a given society, the more they require the care and concern of others, and in particular the intervention of governmental authority. In this way the principle of solidarity … is clearly seen to be one of the fundamental principles of the Christian view of social and political organisation.[45]

But while the state exists to promote, protect and help realise the common good, it is not the only community responsible for the common good. There are many other 'lesser' or 'lower' communities in society which also contribute to the common good. It is important that the state does not hinder or limit the functioning of these communities, assuming of course that their functioning does not harm the common good. This is where the principle of subsidiarity has its place: it limits the state's scope by preserving the rights and duties of individuals, families and other organisations and communities. To quote *Centesimus Annus*: 'The state has the duty of watching over the common good and of ensuring that every sector of social life, not excluding the economic one, contributes to achieving that good, while respecting the rightful autonomy of each sector'.[46] However, the state cannot be expected to solve every problem because the individual, the family and society are prior to the state and the state exists in order to protect their rights and not to stifle them.[47] It is the principle of subsidiarity which ensures that individuals, families and society do not end up being absorbed by the state. Society must be recognised as a complex organism made up of a variety of intermediary groups, beginning with the family. These groups are always called to be geared to the wellbeing of all.

The principle of subsidiarity is taught from the encyclical *Quadragesimo Anno* in 1931 onwards: a community of a higher order should not interfere in the internal life of a community of a lower order.[48] Responsibilities and decisions should be attended to as close as possible to the level of the individual initiative in local communities and institutions. The principle has been much emphasised by Catholic industrialists and is popular today amongst those who are keen to reduce the functions and tasks of the state. This calls for a correction.

The principle of subsidiarity has a corollary, namely the principle of supplementation. This principle requires the state to assist communities, families and individuals to contribute more effectively to the common good. Hence, the state should supplement their activities when the demands of justice exceed their capacities. In other words, when private initiative is inadequate, the state should stimulate, aid and co-ordinate and if necessary, supplement and complete it.

The idea underpinning the principle of supplementation is also to be found in the latest CST encyclical *Centesimus Annus* where it is called the principle of solidarity; it is regarded as a fundamental principle of political organisation.[49] In my view the principle of solidarity takes the principle of supplementation a step further. In the latter the state adds to, helps out and supplements what other groups in society are already doing. The initiative is not with the state. But according to the principle of solidarity the state acts directly on its *own* responsibility for the common good. Examples of such actions mentioned in *Centesimus Annus* are the protection of both human and natural environments 'which cannot be safeguarded simply by market forces',[50] efficient public services,[51] minimum support for the unemployed,[52] and social insurance in old age.[53]

Applying the two principles (of subsidiarity and of solidarity) to the economic sphere *Centesimus Annus* stated:

> The state must contribute to the achievements of these goals both directly and indirectly. Indirectly and according to the principle of subsidiarity, by creating favourable conditions for the free exercise of economic activity. Directly and according to the principle of solidarity by defending the weakest, by placing certain limits on the autonomy of the parties who determine working conditions, and by ensuring in every case the necessary minimum support for the unemployed worker.[54]

The principle of solidarity, when applied to whatever aspect of social, economic and social life, has significant consequences. One such application is to the right of private property. As already mentioned, CST holds that God intended the earth and its resources to be a common gift and therefore all should share in it. This is known as the universal destination of created goods. It does not deny the right of private property which is considered an indispensable condition for the autonomy of the person and the family. But it places private property in the context of solidarity and the common good. Like all other human rights the right to private property is not an absolute right but is circumscribed by the question: what is its effect on the common good? Though intermediate groups have their own autonomy, at the same time they are always to be geared to the wellbeing of all: solidarity must characterise human relations.[55]

Conclusion

This chapter has outlined some of the central themes in CST. Plainly, there is much more that could be said. It should be evident, however, that CST furnishes a rich heritage of thinking on the key social, economic, and political questions which concern the modern world. In formulating their *Social Justice Statement*, the church leaders drew heavily, although by no means exclusively, on CST. Consequently, the *Statement* makes extensive use of concepts like human dignity and the common good, and the principles of subsidiarity and supplementation.

In a recent speech, Pope John Paul II made the following observations about the state and its role:

> The state should be conceived as a service of synthesis, of protection, of orientation for civil society, with respect for it, its initiatives and values; a state based on law together with a social state, which offers everyone the legal guarantees of an orderly existence and assures the most vulnerable the support they need in order not to succumb to the arrogance and indifference of the powerful.[56]

Concerns of this nature were central to the *Social Justice Statement*. My firm hope is that the churches will continue to speak and act on behalf of the vulnerable and constantly challenge those in positions of power to pursue the common good.

Notes

Most of the notes below refer to CST documents. The full titles of these documents are:

CA = *Centesimus Annus – The 100th Year*, John Paul II, 1991.
GS = *Gaudium et Spes – The Pastoral Constitution on the Church in the Modern World*, Second Vatican Council, 1965.
LE = *Laborem Exercens – On Human Work*, John Paul II, 1979.
MM = *Mater et Magistra – Christianity and Social Progress*, John XXIII, 1961.
OA = *Octogesima Adveniens – A Call to Action*, Paul VI, 1971.
PT = *Pacem in Terris – Peace on Earth*, John XXIII, 1963.
QA = *Quadragesimo Anno – On Reconstructing the Social Order*, Pius XI, 1931.
RN = *Rerum Novarum – On the Condition of Labour*, Leo XIII, 1891.
SRS = *Sollicitudo Rei Socialis – The Social Concerns of the Church*, John Paul II, 1987.

1. CA 5; OA 4.
2. CA 57.
3. Rom 12:2.
4. GS 37.2.
5. GS 40.2.
6. GS 39.
7. GS 39.
8. GS 39.1.
9. CA 59.
10. Speech printed in 'Osservatore Romano', 15 September 1993, Vatican.
11. Speech printed in 'Osservatore Romano', 8 September 1993, Vatican.
12. SRS 41.
13. OA 4.
14. MM 229.
15. MM 238.
16. For a more detailed account of the early history of Catholic moral teaching, see Herve Carrier, S.J. *The Social Doctrine of the Church,* Vatican City, 1990.
17. RN 3.
18. QA 110.
19. QA 49.
20. OA 48.1.
21. See Rom 2:15-16.
22. CA 26.
23. SRS 36.
24. Speech printed in 'Osservatore Romano', 28 April 1991, Vatican.
25. CA 11.
26. CA 32 and 33.
27. CA 36 and 41.
28. RN 3.
29. SRS 42.

30. CA 28-31.
31. CA 58.
32. QA 110.
33. SRS 38.
34. CA 47.
35. GS 26 and 74; MM 66.
36. Speech printed in 'Osservatore Romano', 15 September 1993, Vatican.
37. GS 74.2.
38. GS 74.
39. PT 54.
40. GS 74.1; CA 11.
41. GS 26.1.
42. CA 21.
43. CA 47.
44. CA 15.
45. CA 10.
46. CA 11.
47. CA 11.
48. QA 78-80.
49. CA 10.
50. CA 40.
51. CA 48. This is worked out in greater detail in PT 64.
52. CA 15.
53. CA 34.
54. CA 15.
55. MM 65.
56. Speech printed in 'Osservatore Romano', 15 September 1993, Vatican.

Chapter 6

Social Justice and the Treasury Line

Petrus Simons

Introduction

The social philosophy underpinning the *Social Justice Statement* is very different from that which has been guiding public policy in New Zealand, especially in the social policy arena, since the late 1980s. In particular, it stands in marked contrast to the philosophy enunciated by the Treasury. Whereas the *Statement* emphasises the importance of human dignity, social justice, the common good, and human interdependence, the Treasury emphasises individual initiative, private arrangements, voluntary contracts, and allocative efficiency, and stresses the negative economic consequences of income redistribution. While accepting that the state should promote social equity, the Treasury gives less weight to equity considerations than efficiency.

In their *Statement* the church leaders maintain that:

> The commitment to social justice is an essential part of life lived according to the Gospel of Jesus Christ and in response to the prophetic words found in other parts of the Bible. (§.2)

Social justice is said to include:

> ... fairness in the distribution of income, wealth and power in our society ... fairness in the operation of those structures (the social, economic and political structures) so that they enable all citizens to be active and productive participants in the life of society. (§.3)

The latter part of the definition has parallels with the view taken in the *Report of the Royal Commission on Social Security* in 1972 that all citizens, regardless of their socioeconomic status, should be 'able to feel a sense of participation in and belonging to the community'.[1] The church leaders based their approach to social justice on 'the values taught in the Scriptures and embodied in the tradition of the Church' (§.1). Such values and traditions play little role in the Treasury's social philosophy.

The purpose of this chapter is two-fold: first, to outline and critique the foundations of the Treasury's social philosophy; and second, to suggest an alternative conception of the social order based on Christian principles.

A Critique of the Treasury View

Perhaps the best source of the Treasury's views on social justice or equity is that contained in *Government Management.*[2] This document was prepared prior to the 1987 general election as a briefing for the incoming government. It includes a large section setting out a theory of the state (see pp. 9-48). This theory is then applied to a number of issues including social policy. The document is remarkable, not merely in regard to the content of the social and political philosophy it espouses, but also because it is most unusual for government departments to advocate their own political philosophy; such a task is normally left to political parties and philosophers.

In my view, the Treasury's theory of the state is flawed. It supplies a few important bones, but not a whole skeleton, let alone the necessary flesh and blood. The whole discussion is couched in terms of individuals who make economic decisions about the use of resources. The task of the government is reduced to that of an economic agent, be it an agent of the Crown or an agent of taxpayers. There is hardly any discussion, for instance, about democratic theory, the role of citizens, or the pursuit of the public interest. In fact, the Treasury seems to imply that when private individuals are unable to meet their social and economic needs, such problems should be regarded as being of a private rather than a public nature. The existence of such problems does not automatically justify government intervention. As the Treasury puts it:

> Uncontracted-for interdependencies either detrimental or beneficial are what are respectively usually termed social costs or social benefits. They are also frequently said to indicate market failure. However, the reason why these so called social costs or social benefits exist, or why the market is said to fail (that is, there is no contract) is because there

> are costs to putting things right. But to distinguish such uncontracted costs or benefits as social, or as a case of market failure is not useful. These uncontracted-for effects are private. Moreover, the reason why the effect may not be accounted for is that it would be too costly for this accounting to be done. Thus the market can not be said to have failed. People have still weighed benefits against costs and decided not to attempt to correct an effect that is too costly to correct. Given the constraints this is socially beneficial. If these uncontracted-for effects are too costly to put right then society may be better off with them.[3]

Such an approach is open to numerous objections. There is space to consider only a few of these here.

The Limits to Voluntary Contracting

To start with, the assumption that people adjust efficiently to constraints in the absence of state intervention begs many questions about the nature of efficiency, whether individuals are in a position to make informed choices, whether individuals are always the best judges of their own interests, whether the preferences of all individuals should count equally, whether individuals are in a position to assess the costs of the so-called 'uncontracted-for effects', the possibility of system failures, and so on. Equally questionable is the assumption that the state is unable to intervene efficiently and effectively to reduce the social costs of certain kinds of economic activity.

The provision and funding of health care highlights these points. In many cases individuals are not the best judges of what health care interventions they require for their own wellbeing. Also, as the experience of the United States indicates, the funding of health care primarily though private health insurance rather than comprehensive social insurance is both inefficient and inequitable.[4] The key elements of market failure, such as a lack of competition, insufficient or asymmetrical information, inadequate and inequitable access to health care services, the presence of externalities and market disequilibrium, all apply to the health care market in the United States. While health care costs have risen throughout the OECD during the past few decades, the situation in the United States has been worse than elsewhere and has been one of the primary motivations for the Clinton Administration's proposed health reforms. Clearly, voluntarily contracting individuals, assuming they exist, have been unable to prevent this cost escalation. Nor does it seem reasonable to argue that those

Americans who are too poor to purchase health insurance accept the proposition that either they themselves or their society are better off as a result of this cost escalation.

The impression given by *Government Management* is that society is no more than a collection of voluntarily contracting individuals. Likewise, families, churches, trade unions, and the various other institutions of civic society are no more than coalitions of individuals, merely the sum of their parts. From this perspective, a firm is simply a nexus of contracts between resource owners. Meanwhile, individuals are represented as sophisticated computers. They engage continuously in cost-benefit calculations. Marginal costs are compared with marginal benefits and decisions made accordingly. If individuals find the apparatus of the government in their way, they will offer benefits to bureaucrats to improve their own private welfare. They are presumed to have little concern about the welfare of others, the distribution of income or wealth, or the common good.

If we ask what it is that initiates this enormous computing effort, then the simple answer is: scarce resources.

> The basic constraint a society faces is the scarcity of resources (both physical and human) relative to the demands that can be placed upon them ... . Scarcity then is the most fundamental constraint of all.[5]

How should society deal with this constraint? According to the Treasury, 'The solution to the problem of scarce resources is the specification of enforceable rights'.[6] In this context the state plays an essential role by defining and enforcing rights through its monopoly of coercive powers.

Note the similarities of this view to those of the English political philosopher, John Locke (1632-1704). Locke's motivation was inspired by the science/mathematical ideal (see Chapter 2) prevalent in the seventeenth century.[7] From this perspective, the simplest elements of society are individuals. Individuals are born in a state of nature with inalienable rights to life, freedom and property. Property is basic because the land under an individual's control provides the means of existence. Individuals are presumed to come together to agree upon a social contract in order to protect their property. They thereby surrender two rights to the state: the right to do what is necessary for their survival and the right to punish.

Both Locke and the Treasury believe that the state should protect property rights to allow individuals to engage in trade by exchanging property. Property rights provide access to resources by the way of the price mechanism, because such rights provide a basis for buying and selling. These processes are complicated, in the Treasury's view, by four factors: we live in an interdependent world; individuals have bounded rationality inasmuch as they cannot anticipate and foresee all the effects of their actions, which leads to uncertainty; there are costs associated with obtaining information; and people have opportunistic tendencies which are displayed in shirking, free-riding, and rent-seeking behaviour. Individuals have evolved a wide variety of institutions to deal with these complications. According to the Treasury, government intervention is not necessarily better at dealing with them than individuals acting independently via other means. Hence, before recommending governmental intervention it is necessary to undertake a 'comparative systems analysis'. This entails, amongst other things, an analysis of the costs and benefits of each of the available policy options with the aim of choosing the optimal or least-cost solution. It can be surmised, from the drift of the Treasury's discussion, that in most cases voluntary forms of contracting have greater merit than alternative approaches. Voluntary solutions are claimed by the Treasury to be responsive to changes in technology, preferences, and so forth. They also involve 'decentralised decision-making which enables quick adaptations to new information and incentives'.[8]

The Treasury's approach as just described raises at least two issues. Whatever the theoretical merits of the 'comparative systems analysis', it encounters all the problems associated with so-called 'rational' policy analysis and cost-benefit analysis (e.g. limited information, uncertainty, the limited predictive capacity of the social sciences, the problem of measuring and valuing intangibles, the problem of ranking values, etc.). Hence, it is extremely difficult in many cases to ascertain the relative merits of the available policy options. Another problem lies in the fact that a reliance upon markets (or voluntary contracting) necessarily entails a certain partitioning in the domain of choice available to individuals. That is to say, individuals cannot *via market transactions* make certain kinds of choices. For example, they cannot choose whether collective goods such as defence and policing should be provided, or how much should be spent on the provision of collective goods, or the kind of society in which they want to live – such as whether the society should be bicultural or multicultural, just or unjust. Such choices are of a collective and public nature and can only be decided collectively by democratic political institutions. As a consequence, a reliance on voluntary contracting, as preferred by the Treasury, has the effect, intentionally or otherwise, of ruling out many options and precludes the possibility of society making certain kinds of choices. What is more, it necessarily gives priority to individuals' market preferences (as revealed in their purchasing decisions) over their political preferences (as revealed by their voting behaviour). Yet there is no reason to suppose that the preferences that individuals express via the political process are any less legitimate than those expressed in the market. Further, because of inequalities in wealth and income, some individuals have a much greater capacity to participate in the market and to reveal their preferences by way of market transactions. Such considerations receive relatively little attention in the Treasury's analysis.

This leads to a broader issue. From the Treasury's perspective, the state appears to be no more than an instrument for mediating and enforcing private agreements between individuals. It is not seen, therefore, primarily as a means for promoting shared or common interests; in short, the central rationale for the state is to serve private interests rather than the public interest. But such a view is open to serious objections. It suggests that the state is simply a nexus of contracts while laws are merely contracts with many signatories devised to minimise transaction costs. But if this is the case, what is to prevent an individual from withdrawing his or her consent, or refusing to sign up in the first place? Further, as Barry argues, 'A 'public authority' which can act only when all those subject to it are agreed is not a *public* authority at all';[9] it is merely a servant of private individuals.

Equity, Taxation and Targeting

The idea of trade-offs between values, especially between efficiency and equity, is central to the Treasury's approach:[10]

> By interfering too much in the income received by owners the government may adversely affect incentives to efficiently allocate and use scarce resources. The necessity to evaluate trade-offs between efficiency and equity cannot be over-emphasised. The same is true when trade-offs exist between other objectives.[11]

The Treasury considers some of these objectives when discussing the negative effects of taxation:

> Taxation creates disincentives to work and invest, and it encourages economically wasteful activities aimed at avoiding tax. The equity effects depend on what one does with the taxes collected. Whether they are given back to the individual or not. If they are, then given the

> costs of taxation and expenditure, it may be better to consider tax credits or tax rebates to the individuals concerned rather than become involved in churning [i.e., some income groups pay taxes and then receive back welfare benefits].[12]

Unfortunately, no empirical work to justify these statements is presented. There is a view, however, which says that many people on higher incomes do not mind paying tax. In any event, it should be borne in mind that income tax levels in New Zealand are low by international standards, with a top marginal rate of only 33 per cent. Moreover, many countries with much higher top income tax rates (e.g. Japan and Germany) have enjoyed higher rates of economic growth than New Zealand during the past few decades. Hence, one may be forgiven for having doubts about the Treasury's claims.

Generally, according to the Treasury, centralised state control is problematic, inasmuch as it:

> ... may crowd out private arrangements with consequent losses in flexibility, diversity and the evolutionary capacities of social organisations. This is particularly visible where state-funded social services, or consumer protection legislation reduces the amount private individuals invest in market or self-insurance (for example, for old age).[13]

The views summarised make it plain that we cannot expect enthusiastic Treasury support for a strongly progressive income tax system, substantial income redistribution, or universal systems of social assistance. Indeed, *Government Management* reveals a clear preference for means-testing income assistance because it allows a reduction in overall tax levels. This approach is not without problems.[14] For example, targeted forms of social assistance inevitably give rise to situations where recipients lose some of their state support as their private income rises. This typically results in high effective marginal tax rates. The groups most affected tend to be those on low-to-modest incomes. Another problem with means-testing is that those receiving income assistance are not encouraged to make their own arrangements. They have an incentive to reduce their work effort and to save less.

These paradoxes of means-testing were readily apparent in the debate in 1993-1994 over the application of an assets test to those in long-term geriatric care. Surely, the prospect of a 90-100 per cent tax rate on such individuals' assets is likely to be a disincentive to save during their working life.

Comprehensive assets testing is also very intrusive. Such disincentives and intrusiveness, of course, are the exact opposite of the outcomes sought by those, such as the Treasury, concerned to protect individuals' property rights.

It is implied in the Treasury's thinking that as soon as a country has the right set of microeconomic relationships, with the smallest possible state, then unemployment will fall substantially. Real wages will adjust (downwards) to the point where the labour market clears. But the labour market rarely works as suggested by simple neo-classical models of demand and supply. For one thing, the application of new technologies reduces the demand for labour and changes the requirements for skills and education in a very dynamic way and over a period of time. Individual market suppliers are not well placed to assess these needs in order to make decisions as to how they are to be met in the way of retraining and other educational services.

The evidence suggests that policy prescriptions of the kind recommended by the Treasury and implemented by recent governments are likely to produce greater social and economic inequality. It is thus no surprise that there has been growing inequality of income distribution in New Zealand during the past decade or so.[15] Especially at a time of high unemployment, a growing gap between rich and poor is destructive of a society's cohesion.

Other Problems with the Treasury's View

In the Treasury's view, humanity is essentially the economic 'man' of classical economic theory who stands as the model for the individual. It is an abstraction in which the many diverse functions of humanity (rational, social, economic, aesthetic, ethical, etc.) are subsumed by just one of them – the economic. The world, also, is represented only in terms of its economic value, a value solely expressed in material terms. Such views are typical of Western thinking inasmuch as they place economic 'man' in opposition to the world as an accumulator and exploiter of its resources.

Underlying this view are unarticulated assumptions concerning the role of technology. The exploitation of resources resulting in the production of a flow of goods and services is by means of technology which is designed on the basis of scientific discoveries. So powerful is the drive for technological innovation that there is a tendency in modern society for economic and technological powers to develop without adequate controls over them. Globalisation means that national governments have less and less control over their economies. Capital flows to where unit labour costs are least and that tends to be in the third world, where environmental standards tend to be lax. Underlying the Treasury's approach is the view that the development of technology in the pursuit of wealth via the market is an unalloyed good. But this ignores the harmful social effects which technological development often produces.

It is striking that the Treasury's contracting individual suffers from what is called bounded rationality. Nobody can perfectly anticipate all the effects of his or her actions. Nobody has a perfect insight into the future. Thus, individuals experience uncertainty. The evidence suggests that many people do not act wisely when confronted with uncertainty, particularly uncertainty surrounding their long-term future interests. This results in people both under-and over-insuring themselves in areas like the provision of health care and retirement income. Whereas '[i]ndividuals may tell themselves, one by one, that "it will never happen to me", public officials know that it will happen to some of them'.[16] In some cases, therefore, governments can do things better than individuals acting independently.

The Treasury's political philosophy is founded upon some of the basic premises of Western culture. One of these is the idea of freedom or liberty, in particular freedom from state interference. The Treasury acknowledges that freedom has both negative and positive aspects: it requires both the absence of constraints (negative liberty) as well as the capacity and resources for individuals to act (positive liberty). However, it tends to emphasise the need to minimise state interference in the interests of maximising negative liberty rather than ensuring greater equality of opportunity in the interests of promoting positive liberty. To the extent that it stresses positive liberty, it is the liberty of contractors in the market place. Further, the Treasury tends to ignore the coercive role which non-state bodies (such as firms) can exercise in various spheres of life.

Last, the Treasury's cavalier attitude to economic management should be remarked upon. It appears to consider this almost entirely in terms of financial flows rather than in terms of managing the economy's long-term resource use. Thus, since 1985 New Zealand has had a macroeconomic policy which has systematically dampened the real economy because the government increased one basic relative price (i.e. the rate of foreign exchange) beyond the level at which there could be a reasonable rate of output growth. It has done this basically through the monetary policy of the Reserve Bank. Related to this policy is the phenomenon that since 1985 the real rate of interest has been higher than the rate of real GDP growth. In simple terms this means that there is not enough output growth to cover the costs of capital invested to produce higher output. This dampens capital investment in the economy.

By systematically reducing government expenditures, by forcing tax rates down and by having a relatively flat tax structure, in combination with a slow-growing real economy, the stage has been set for a rise in the wealth of higher income groups (they are much less likely to lose their jobs), whilst the low income groups suffer declining real incomes. Unemployment is unlikely to reduce much under this scenario. By allowing a high level of unemployment, an indirect asset test on marginalised people is applied. Those who are unemployed for long periods of time, for instance, are damaged in their human dignity as they are deprived of a vocation. Moreover, given current benefit levels, their income is such that their asset base will tend to fall over time. It can be argued that this damage to the self-esteem of the unemployed contributes to a range of other problems such as suicide, abortion, prostitution, and euthanasia. The growing application of income and asset testing to health and education will also have the effect of reducing people's resource base and thus of widening the gap between rich and poor. In turn, this will exacerbate the unemployment problem. Hence, I have no hesitation in calling the Treasury-inspired policies anti-life.

There Are Alternatives

If we take the concept of public justice (see Chapter 2) as our starting point, it is possible to devise an economic and social strategy very different from that advanced by the Treasury. To start with, it must be recognised that society is made up of a wide range of social institutions and structures in which individuals interact in many different ways (e.g. families, clubs, schools, business enterprises, churches, etc.). One of the responsibilities of the state must be to ensure that such institutions are able to flourish and meet the needs of their members and the wider community. In this context, the principle of subsidiarity, as mentioned in the *Social Justice Statement*, is of considerable importance (see Chapters 2 and 5).

Another responsibility of the state is to ensure that inequalities in the distribution of wealth and income are not excessive. This implies that the tax system should be reasonably progressive rather than proportional or regressive. It also implies that there should be inheritance taxes and taxes on wealth. None of these requirements is currently met in New Zealand.

Equally important, the state has a responsibility to minimise unemployment. Indeed, one of the litmus tests of the success or otherwise of a government's economic and social policies is the level of unemployment. Not only should macroeconomic policies be adjusted to promote employment, within the constraints of the balance of payments, but also the network of social relationships should be enhanced and enlarged to provide a wider range of employment opportunities. In addition, environmental policy should be integrated in general policy formulation.

As far as social assistance programmes are concerned, preference should be given to universal systems rather than means-tested forms of assistance. Income-tests and asset-tests tend to be intrusive, they often impose significant economic disincentives, they frequently entail high administrative and compliance costs (per dollar of assistance), and do not always yield substantial fiscal savings. Admittedly, universal social welfare systems will always be used by 'free-riders' to some extent. Such a cost, however, is minor compared with the benefit of much greater respect for human dignity and ease of administration.

The *Social Justice Statement* hints at these principles when its refers to fairness (i) in the distribution of income, wealth and power in our society, (ii) in the social, economic and political structures we have created, and (iii) in the operation of those structures so that they enable all citizens to be active and productive participants in the life of society.

To illustrate, consider the problem of unemployment. There is plenty of work to be done such that if it were all attempted there would be a shortage rather than an excess of labour supply at present. Currently, many types of work are currently not regarded as work or else are undervalued. This includes caring for the aged, the handicapped, the unemployed, and the young.

It should be possible to develop sets of new networks which re-employ the unemployed. To facilitate this, macroeconomic policy would need to be altered. The government would have to initiate more capital spending. It could also provide endowment capital to corporations which aim to develop new services to be run by unemployed people. A recent example of this is a corporation in Rotterdam set up to buy a parking building which had been abandoned because it had been subjected to vandalism and thuggery. The corporation bought the building. It provided supervision around the clock and developed a range of services for those parking their cars such as car-washing, shopping, servicing cars, and so forth. Schemes of this type can be developed to tackle urban revitalisation, control noxious weeds and animals, set up service centres in suburbs where many old people live, and provide special youth centres, perhaps in conjunction with the rehabilitation of drug victims. To enable such activities to be funded, government spending would have to be increased. By means of a more progressive tax system and a wider tax base, a redistribution towards the lower income groups, including the unemployed, is possible without a major impact on the fiscal deficit.

Unemployment and poverty are highly demoralising and traumatising, and are implicated in a range of social problems. If we are to be keepers of our sisters and brothers, we cannot be at peace with such developments. The apparatus of the state should be used to alleviate and as far as possible reduce unemployment. As indicated above, this can be done in a more constructive way than by just dishing out dole payments. If done wisely, the whole community will benefit.

Conclusion

Underlying the *Social Justice Statement* is a concern for the social effects of government economic and social policy – unemployment, poverty, etc. Such concern is completely at variance with the Treasury's line of thinking which has shaped so much of that policy in recent years. This chapter has analysed and criticised some of the key assumptions of the Treasury's philosophy as expressed in the influential *Government Management* briefing papers. In its place an alternative approach has been offered more in sympathy with the concerns of the *Statement.* Finally, the chapter has provided suggestions as to the ways in which such an approach can be put into practice.

Notes

1. *Report of the Royal Commission on Social Security,* Wellington: Government Printer, 1972, p. 65.
2. The Treasury, *Government Management*, Volume 1, Wellington: Government Printer, 1987.
3. Ibid., pp. 28-29.
4. S. Mirmirani and R.N. Spivack, 'Health Care System Collapse in the United States: Capitalist Market Failure!', *De Economist*, 141/3, 1993, pp. 419-31.
5. The Treasury, *Government Management*, p. 11.
6. Ibid., p. 13.
7. J.P.A. Mekkes, John Locke, in *Baanbrekers van het Humanisme*, T. Wever, Franeker, no year.
8. The Treasury, *Government Management*, p. 23.
9. Brian Barry, *Political Argument*, London: Routledge and Kegan Paul, 1965, p. 256.
10. For a critique of the notion that equity and efficiency must be traded against each other see H. Hovenkamp, 'Positivism in Law and Economics', *California Law Review*, 78/4, 1990, pp. 815-52, esp. p. 847ff.
11. Ibid., p. 33.
12. Ibid., p. 37.
13. Ibid., p. 46.

14. See Jonathan Boston, 'Targetting: Social Assistance for All or Just for the Poor?' in J. Boston and P. Dalziel, (eds), *The Decent Society? Essays in Response to National's Economic and Social Policies* Auckland: Oxford University Press, 1992, pp. 76-99.
15. Petrus Simons, 'Tunnel or Tree: Social Justice in a Technistic Society', private paper 1993.
16. R.E. Goodin, 'Liberalism and the Best-Judge Principle, *Political Studies*, 38, 1990, p. 190.

Contributors

Jonathan Boston is Associate Professor of Public Policy at Victoria University of Wellington. In recent years he has undertaken research in a number of fields, including aspects of social policy, higher education policy, public sector reform, and moral theology. His most recent books include *Reshaping the State* (co-edited, Oxford University Press, 1991) and *The Decent Society? Essays in Response to National's Economic and Social Policies* (co-edited, Oxford University Press, 1992).

Alan Cameron is Senior Lecturer in Commercial Law at Victoria University of Wellington. He holds a Master of Laws in Jurisprudence from Victoria University. He has written articles on aspects of legal philosophy and is currently secretary of the Association for Christian Scholarship and Treasurer of the New Zealand Society for Legal and Social Philosophy.

Christopher Marshall is Head of the Department of New Testament Studies at the Bible College of New Zealand in Auckland. He holds a doctorate in New Testament from London University, and is author of *Faith as a Theme in Mark's Narrative* (Cambridge University Press, 1989), *Kingdom Come: The Kingdom of God in the Teaching of Jesus* (Impetus Press, 1993), and several articles on ethical and biblical subjects.

Ruth Smithies is Project Assistant to the Archbishop of Wellington, Cardinal Tom Williams, and is also responsible for the Archdiocesan Office for Justice, Peace and Development. She assisted the church leaders with the drafting of the *Social Justice Statement* in 1993, and co-edited the companion volume *Making Choices: Social Justice for Our Times*. She holds a doctorate in theology from the University of Amsterdam, and undertook post-doctoral studies in Assyriology at the Institute for the Ancient Near East, University of Leiden.

Petrus Simons is an economist with Integrated Economic Services in Wellington. He holds an MCA in economics from Victoria University of Wellington, and has worked for various organisations including the New Zealand Employers Federation and the BNZ. He has written various articles on economic issues and social ethics, and has translated and edited *The Future: Our Choice or God's Gift* (Exile Publications, 1990), and co-edited *Down to Earth: The Mission of the Church in Secular Society* (Exile Publications, 1994).

Index

Qns

- Constitution — wd.
- Power / coercion
- Gender — & the state (i.e. position of polity?) → promote a certain sort of totality
- Freedom
- nature of the person < corporate / wd.
- epistemology.

"Foundationalism"

↓

ad hoc

& lack of awareness of how debateable & culture bound views are —

good at analyzing deficiencies; analyzing complexity; __, few answers?

— cannot view of the state [wrong]

— with repeating candour & humility —
The contributors are v. conscious
of the difficulty & complexity
of our tasks

~~Uy at attack~~ is quite, even at times extremely, pluralized. Diff soldiers & diff weapons are marching under the same banner.

Yet, in this case, they are all also marching in basically the same direction, and in view of the evident drawing, this unity is opp^n to RW ideology, the NR, current Treasury policy, & the Nat. Govts extension of Rogernomics, is ~~highly~~ the now significant

---

The missing figure — { Smith (& the [illegible]?) Tovrmer Calvin Cornish —

p. 189

Underlying the book is a methodological, which is to say, a theological pluralism ← a significant aspect & a sad aspect —